S T U D E I   R I E   S

Successful teamwork!

STUDENT-FRIENDLY GUIDES

Successful teamwork!

for undergraduates and taught postgraduates
working on group projects

PETER LEVIN

Open University Press

Open University Press
McGraw-Hill Education
McGraw-Hill House
Shoppenhangers Road
Maidenhead
Berkshire
England
SL6 2QL

email: enquiries@openup.co.uk
world wide web: www.openup.co.uk

and Two Penn Plaza, New York, NY 10121-2289, USA

First published 2005

A catalogue record of this book is available from the British Library

ISBN 0 335 21578 5

Library of Congress Cataloging-in-Publication Data
CIP data applied for

Typeset by YHT Ltd, London
Printed in the UK by Bell & Bain Ltd, Glasgow

Contents

Part Four: Perspectives on team behaviour

Part Five: Teamwork issues and solutions

Part Six: Benefiting from the experience

List of Tables

List of Boxes

Teamwork in universities:

READ THIS FIRST!

Are you a university student who finds yourself expected to do some of your academic work in a group, or even a 'team', with other students? If so, this book is for you. It is designed to support you through the experience and to help you deal with the many issues that inevitably arise in working with other people. It is especially for students who have been 'thrown in at the deep end': formed into groups, assigned a project, and then left alone to get on with it rather than being provided with support for working in this way.

In recent years 'teamwork' has become a buzzword in UK higher education. Central government has put 'employability' on its HE agenda. In many universities senior managers and academics have noticed that employers and employers' organizations very often put 'teamwork' at or near the head of the list of skills they want graduate recruits to possess, and have been asking what their institutions can do to ensure that students gain this skill. And teachers in HE are increasingly giving their students projects to carry out in groups as part of their curriculum work.

There is something incongruous in all this. The culture of UK secondary and higher education is deeply infused with an ethos of individual achievement. It's an ethos that's almost diametrically opposite to that of teamwork. Teamwork is for the sports field, not the classroom. When it comes to academic work, it's everyone for himself or herself. You take exams as an individual, not as a member of a team; you gain admission to university as an individual, not as a member of a team. Your educational experience could not have been more effective in getting you to take it for granted that academic work is a solitary pursuit if it had been designed for that purpose.

At university, academics – themselves appointed and promoted on the basis of their individual prowess, chiefly in research – play their part in maintaining this culture. So when you are told by your teachers that you're required to 'do' teamwork, you are getting a message that is at odds with those they've given you up to now. You may indeed get *mixed* messages, if on the one hand you are told that on projects you must work in teams with other students but on the other that if you collaborate with other students in writing tasks, such collaboration will be treated as collusion and severely punished!

You may well find that your teachers don't comprehend that when they require you to work in teams they are asking you to do something that is completely contrary to the prevailing academic culture and ethos, and that they offer you no help whatever in dealing with the conflicting pressures that you're under. They may themselves be experts in their field, but this does not mean that they are experts in working with other people. Indeed, their own immersion in the ethos of individual achievement may have had the result that their experience of working with other people is minimal.

There is evidence, anecdotal but widespread, that academics' usual practice is to form students into groups (or let them select their own), give them their assignment, and leave them to it. If they do provide assistance, it is primarily to do with the substance of the project, not with the process of working together. To be fair, the pressures on academics to teach, carry out research and undertake administrative duties are so great nowadays that all but the most dedicated will be inhibited from trying to become a 'teamwork tutor' too. But the consequence is that you have to learn for yourself how to be a member of a team.

Interestingly, learning to work in a team is a very different process from that of academic learning, and this again raises questions to do with the culture of higher education. Academic learning is in a sense a 'second-hand' experience, assimilating observations, insights, theories and explanations, ideas and critiques put forward by other people, through the medium of – in particular – the written word and the spoken word, via books and articles and web pages, and the lectures that academics give. But learning teamwork is an 'experiential' process: you learn at first hand, through your own experience, as you do in the real world.

My aim in writing this book is to provide you with a guide to working creatively and constructively on a project as a member of a team, even if the academic environment is not supportive. It draws heavily on my own experience of providing 'teamwork tutoring' support for groups of students undertaking projects in a range of subjects. The emphasis is on practical help, as you can see from the question-and-answer approach of the book and the list of issues addressed in Part Five. Where I bring in theoretical perspectives, it is with the aim of helping you to make sense of the experiences you're having or have had in the team context.

But I'm not losing sight of the employability dimension. There is no doubt that employers large and small are today looking to recruit people who will work well with others: in project teams, on task forces, on day-to-day operations, liaising across departments, and so on. And in the recruitment process itself you are likely to find yourself faced with group exercises and to be asked about your experiences of teamwork. In Part Six you will find suggestions that will help you to do justice to yourself in these situations.

Part One

Basics

and context

In this part of the book my aim is to get some of the basics out of the way –
What do we mean by 'a team'? What are the benefits of working in a team?
– and make some suggestions as to the skills that can be acquired by working
in a team. I show how experience of academic teamwork is relevant to the
job market and the 'world of work', and how teamwork skills come into play
in various types of team project.

What do we mean by 'a team'?

*What do you mean by 'a team'?
How can I recognize a team when
I see one or when I'm in one?*

There are nearly as many definitions of 'team' as there are books on teamwork. My offering is as follows. When you first meet the other people you'll be working with, you're a group, not a team. You don't become a team until you have developed methods of working together and relationships have formed between you, i.e. through your collaboration you have begun to 'bond' and develop 'team spirit'. If these collaborative relationships don't (yet) exist, what you're in is a group. Even if you first came together as a self-selected group of friends, that doesn't make you a team. And some groups remain nothing more than groups. Observe a group of students who have been given a project to do. If they start by dividing up the overall task into individual tasks for each of them, then go their separate ways to tackle their individual tasks and don't come together again until they meet to put their respective contributions together, what you have observed is only a group: they did not develop collaborative relationships, they did not develop into a team.

But perhaps the group you are observing meets once or twice a week from the start and communicates between meetings, with everyone pooling their ideas and feeling able to criticize ideas constructively, keeping an eye on how individual tasks are progressing, and helping each other with them in various ways. There may be disagreements, perhaps heated at times, but when they are getting on with the work the atmosphere is purposeful and good-humoured. These are indicators of collaborative relationships. This group has become a team.

There are different kinds of teams. In particular, an academic team is different from a sports team in one important respect. Where the central activity is physical, as in the case of a sport, team members work together at the same time, and in close proximity, and are mutually dependent. Where the central activity is intellectual, there will be some events that have all these characteristics, such as brainstorming meetings where people 'spark off' one another, but the general pattern of work will be one where people come together, then separate to undertake their individual tasks, come together again, then separate again, and so on. And the crucial activity, thinking, is one that takes place inside your own head, and in that respect *must* be an individual activity, not a collective one. But you can get the same kind of bonding, exhilaration and mutual support and appreciation in an academic team as in a sports team.

The benefits of working in a team

What will I get from working in a team?

From an employability point of view, the experience of working in a team – assuming that you've learned something from it – will stand you in good stead in the world of work, both in applying for jobs and afterwards, when you find yourself placed in a team and having to adjust to it. But there can be more immediate benefits too: ones that are relevant to studying.

Especially if it has been a good experience, one benefit that you'll get from working in a team is that it will give you a wider appreciation of 'learning'. You'll see that the ability to work creatively and effectively in a team is a 'skill for learning' as well as a 'skill for employability'. Not only will you learn from other students, you'll discover that when it comes to learning the whole is greater than the sum of the parts. This way of working will also demonstrate to you – or remind you – how effective (and enjoyable) learning can be when it is a social experience too.

On team projects you will also have to develop a way of thinking that is different from that put over to you in textbooks and lectures of the conventional academic kind. It is an *issue-oriented* way of thinking. It focuses not on phenomena or themes but on issues: 'How shall we ...?', 'What do we need to do to ...?', 'How can we deal with the situation where ...?' In addressing these issues, you and your fellow students are forced to confront questions of judgment and values, risk, and quality of information, and to cope with the absence of an unique 'right answer'.

And working in teams gives you a very different learning experience from lectures and classes/seminars and individual work on essays or dissertations. Team assignments add variety to the curriculum, and they can also offer you an opportunity to integrate materials from a variety of taught courses: 'integrative' perspectives and skills are well worth developing.

Finally, after participating in a team effort many students report that it has enhanced their self-confidence. Not a bad by-product.

I already have practical experience of teamwork. What can working in a team on an academic assignment add to that?

There are three points to make here. First, there is always scope for improvement: we may be brilliant at some teamwork skills but lag behind at others. Second, at the same time as acquiring useful skills we are likely to have acquired unhelpful habits: a propensity to react to a challenge by becoming angry or withdrawing, for example. Working in a team gives you an opportunity to address these.

Third, no teamwork experience exactly replicates a previous one. The task, the context and/or the people you're working with are different. So even if you already have experience of working in a team you'll have something to learn. If you do have previous experience, that's great. You'll learn a lot by seeing how your new experience compares with previous ones. The challenge for you is to develop further, in particular to develop your facilitative skills and help your fellow team members to give of their best.

(What your previous experience doesn't do, though, is entitle you to be the leader of the new team that you find yourself in. If you take that attitude you'll be fostering hierarchy and creating resentment within the team, and this will make it very difficult for a 'social infrastructure' to develop that is appropriate to the assignment and to the range of human resources that the team members bring to it.)

I'd rather do it by myself, thank you

Certainly it's often simpler to deal with a task on your own. You don't have to negotiate or fit in with anyone else; no questions arise as to someone not pulling their weight. But some students are so steeped in the culture of individual achievement, so used to working on their own, that they can't envisage working in a team with others. They may be reluctant to be placed in a position where they are dependent on the cooperation of others and not in sole control of the eventual product. Or they may simply feel they can do a better job on their own if left alone to get on with it.

If this applies to you, remember that you've been asked to do a group project for a number of reasons. It's not just a matter of seeing if you're capable of producing a good product. It's also a matter of giving you the valuable experience of working with others, and you will learn something from it even if they aren't as clever and experienced as you. And if you can't bear to give up some of your dearly held autonomy, it's probably time that you confronted this aspect of your character rather than indulged it. Give it your best shot!

What are the benefits of teamwork in the 'world of work'?

In the 'world of work' (please note that in using this expression, I don't mean to imply that work does not take place in universities), there are jobs to do that require more time and effort, knowledge, skills, ways of thinking, ideas and flexibility than one person alone can bring to them. And in today's competitive, complex and rapidly changing world, organizations structured as hierarchies – with the people at the top taking decisions and the people at the bottom simply doing what they are told – are like dinosaurs: they cannot survive. Similarly, organizations structured as collections of empires – with separate departments having their own objectives and no incentive to communicate with one another – have a built-in inability to respond to changing circumstances. Teamwork, both on a large scale and small, is widely seen as a better way of organizing affairs, in organizations of all kinds.

Teamwork skills

What skills am I supposed to acquire by working on a project in a team?

Trying to come up with a list of teamwork skills is like trying to come up with a recipe for conducting your life: there are so many ingredients. We can divide these skills into two groups, 'intellectual' and 'emotional'. In Box 1 I offer a list of intellectual skills and in Box 2 a list of emotional skills.

Intellectual skills involve thinking rather than emotions, intuition or instinct. They call for dispassionate observation, investigation and theorizing in analysing the overall task, breaking it down into individual, component tasks, and formulating a plan for carrying them out. Similar skills are required for monitoring progress and identifying action that needs to be taken when things are not going according to plan.

Box 1

Intellectual teamwork skills

- The ability to 'appreciate' a situation: to use observation, investigation and theorizing to identify the salient features, the significant variables and their interconnections, the politically sensitive aspects, and organizational constraints and rewards.
- The ability to think in an 'issue-oriented' way (centring on the need and scope for action) and formulate objectives and proposals for action.
- The ability to plan and manage a project by which to implement proposals.
- The ability to gather and manage knowledge and expertise relevant to one's speciality.
- The ability to deploy other forms of learning alongside 'studying', e.g. imitation, trial-and-error, systematic experiential learning (the plan–do–review cycle).

Students who are working on a reasonably meaty project can develop further intellectual skills, including:

- The ability to identify issues and 'go to the heart' of them.
- The ability to make objectives and constraints explicit, and to formulate 'what would happen if …?' scenarios.
- The ability to plan and manage programmes of work of other kinds besides 'one-off' projects.

Emotional skills involve dealing with your own emotions and establishing relationships with other people. So they include, among others, the skills of developing 'rapport' with other people, of negotiating and resolving differences of opinion with others, of maintaining your own and other people's morale, and not least that of preserving your sanity when faced with a crisis.

Box 2

Emotional teamwork skills

- The ability to communicate both intellectually and emotionally with other team members, to establish rapport with them, to see things from other people's points of view and 'get on the same wavelength' with them. This ability is an essential ingredient of teamwork.

- The ability to communicate one's opinion in a way that respects the feelings of others, e.g. by asking 'what can we learn?' rather than 'who is to blame?', and similarly to listen: to receive the opinions of others in a constructive rather than 'raised hackles' way.

- The ability to negotiate constructively and creatively with, and to mediate between, others.

- The ability to negotiate commitments to carrying out tasks that are realistic in terms of time and practicality.

- The ability to keep the 'social infrastructure' of the team in good repair, by attending to the linkages (communication, trust etc.) between the various members of the team, and thereby helping to ensure that no member becomes isolated.

- The ability to exercise leadership by keeping the team focused on its goal and mobilizing consent for decisive action when necessary.

- The ability to sense crucial needs of the team at particular points in time and respond (e.g. by doing practical things that will contribute to the team's morale and ultimate success).

- The ability to facilitate the making of contributions by other members of the team.

- The ability to participate comfortably in collective activities (such as brainstorming).

- Managerial awareness, e.g. of the importance of planning and managing the task, of time management, and of how a task can be divided into sub-tasks, in relation to the available human resources.

- Readiness to take responsibility, not only for one's particular contribution to the greater task but also for the whole enterprise and for assisting a colleague who is having difficulty.

● Sensitivity to the motivations, expectations and psychological needs of yourself and other members of the team, and the ability to reconcile conflicting ones (e.g. wanting both to be a loyal member of the team and to have maximum control over your own work).

● The ability to reflect on and make sense of the experience of working in a team, to 'reframe' experiences (see them in a different light) and to formulate lessons for the future and to communicate them persuasively.

● A 'feel', based on a combination of theory and experience, for the mechanisms that can be found operating within groups and teams (e.g. the mechanisms by which a 'group' develops into a 'team') and for the ways in which organizational and other constraints can help or hinder a team's effectiveness, and the ability to make use of this attribute.

● A sense of self sufficiently robust to withstand the knocks and turbulence inevitably encountered when working in a team.

How can I learn teamwork skills?

Intellectual teamwork skills can be taught by a teacher to students in a classroom and 'embedded' by using them on a project. Emotional teamwork skills are a different matter. Most such skills are acquired and refined through 'learning experiences' that involve more than the exercise of intellect: they involve feelings. People may feel frustrated and angry with one another, or exhilarated when a team is working well together; they may get carried away on a tide of enthusiasm; morale may go up and down. These experiences take place in the context of a particular situation, and the learning is very much context-dependent. (Every situation we find ourselves in will be different in at least some respects from ones that we've encountered previously, so there will always be something to be learned from it.)

It follows that the process by which we learn emotional teamwork skills is one of 'experiential learning'. Think of it as a three-stage cycle: (1) plan; (2) do; (3) review. And the cycle is reiterative (as cycles are!): the results of your review inform your next plan, and so the cycle begins again.

'Review' is crucial to learning from your experiences. You'll need to get into the habit of asking yourself some questions. How did I feel when I was doing it? How do I feel about it now? What went well? What didn't go so well? What should I do differently next time? These questions may feel awkward at first – personal reflection often leads to self-criticism and it can be painful and embarrassing – but after a while they'll become second nature to you and you'll be able to treat them philosophically. (Some useful expressions: 'You win some, you lose some!' 'Charge it up to experience!')

If you're fortunate, you will get some assistance from your teachers. But their role will necessarily be different from their role in the classroom. They can't be merely instructors. If they are to help you in developing your emotional skills they have to be 'facilitators', people who will help you to realize for yourself – rather than inform you – what there is to be learned from a situation.

Interestingly, there is often a 'game' element in the exercise of emotional skills when it comes to relationships with other people. To undertake activities such as persuasion, negotiation and bargaining is to take part in a 'game' with other people where the prize is getting as much as possible of what you want while maintaining good relationships with the other 'players'. A good facilitator will help to 'shape' the game, to maintain and enhance its value as a learning experience.

As you will appreciate, interpersonal activities such as persuasion, negotiation and bargaining often raise ethical issues, as indicated by the pejorative terms that may be used to describe them: 'taking advantage' of other people, or 'being manipulative'. A good facilitator will be alert to issues of these kinds, will notice when they arise, and will intervene where necessary to help you to develop the skills required in dealing with them.

If you haven't got a facilitator keeping an eye on you, however, don't despair. There is much that you can do for yourself, whether on your own or in your group, as you will see from the following pages.

Academic teamwork and the job market

Aren't teams of students artificial? In their future employment – in 'the world of work' – any team would have an appointed leader: these teams are leaderless.

First of all, it is frequently the case in the world of work, especially in situations that are novel or changing rapidly, that task forces or working parties are assembled where either there is no designated leader or there are a number of lines of accountability connecting members to their parent organizations or departments, not a single line running upwards from 'the leader'. So leaderless teams, made up of people of equal status, are not so unrealistic as might at first appear.

Secondly, students invariably find, when their teams are working effectively, that different members take the lead at different stages of the work, over different tasks and when different issues arise. Team working in the academic context provides an excellent opportunity to observe this phenomenon as well as being part of it. In future employment, a team leader who has had this experience should be sufficiently confident to be able to let different members of his or her team take the lead when they are the ones with relevant expertise or knowledge, rather than feeling that it's the team leader's job to exercise authority and be 'the leader' in all situations.

Will working in a team at uni help me get a job when I graduate, and to progress in my career?

Reports on surveys of employers invariably put 'teamwork skills' high on the list of required attributes of graduate recruits. But does this mean that they want more than the ability and preparedness to 'fit in' and do what they're told without complaining? Evidence is patchy, and the jury is out on this question, but there are clear indications that graduate recruiters who watch candidates tackling team exercises in assessment centres are actively looking for people who are good at establishing rapport with others and seeing their point of view, at drawing out other people's contributions and listening carefully to them, and at 'picking up the ball and running with it'. In Part Six of this book you'll find a section, 'Group exercises in assessment centres', which should help you to apply what you've learned from working on a team project when you're put in a group setting as part of a graduate recruitment exercise.

Part Two

Getting started

With any new team, it is really important to start off on the right foot. In this part of the book I deal with issues around the formation of groups, the process of getting to know one another, and the formulation of 'ground rules', which in my experience are enormously helpful to the effective functioning of teams. I also address questions to do with resources and motivations, and the initial stages of planning your work.

Get in your groups

I'd prefer to choose who I work with. Does that make me a bad person?

How should groups be selected? Ideally selection should be made by academics rather than by students themselves. You will have enough to deal with without being made to feel responsible for other students being excluded, or guilty if you have argued for the inclusion in your own team of someone who subsequently doesn't get on with another member or members. If two of you have got together to choose the other members, you may find yourselves starting off with a 'core' sub-group plus peripheral members. And students who find themselves among the last to be picked are likely to find the selection process a bruising, confidence-sapping experience.

It's probably best for your teachers to make the selection using agreed criteria: a balance of men and women, a mixture of people of different ages and experience, and a mixture of people from different parts of the world. Alternatively, they could employ a random selection process, like drawing lots.

Our teachers have told us to form teams by ourselves. How can we do that without hurting people's feelings?

If your teachers don't take responsibility for the selection process, why don't you all – i.e. the whole year-group – get together and choose a random method and apply it? Draw lots, or alternatively shuffle yourselves around the room, form yourselves into a line or a circle, then number yourselves off from 1 to n, 1 to n, etc., where n is the number of groups. Then all the 1s get in a group, all the 2s, and so on.

What is the ideal group size? I have found that groups of five people work well. The odd number assists in taking decisions if it comes to a vote. With larger groups there is the danger that less assertive people will find it difficult to find their place and make a worthwhile contribution. With only three or four, there may not be enough variety in the group.

I've been put in a group with people I hardly know. Should I try to get transferred?

Being in a mixed team is nothing to be afraid of. Experience has shown that if groups are thoroughly mixed, so that sub-groups (e.g. of particular ethnic or language groups) are not formed, the results can be positively beneficial. Not only do you learn about cultures other than your own; you find ways of addressing and getting over cultural differences. And it can even allow you to try out being a different sort of person, something that it's difficult to do if you're among people who have known you for some time. So it may be scary at first, but it can turn out to be a lot of fun, or even a life-changing experience, later.

I've been put in a group with someone I do know and whom I don't like.

In the world of work you may well find yourself assigned to a team that includes one or more people you do not particularly like. They may or may not particularly like you! Nevertheless you will all be expected to work together. Later on I make some suggestions for managing the situation. Meanwhile, bear in mind that the ability to work with someone you've taken a dislike to is actually a skill worth developing. And sometimes we do change our opinion of people as we get to know them better.

Last year I had a relationship with another student in my year. It ended with me getting dumped. Now I find to my horror that we're both in the same group for a project. How can I get a transfer?

You have my sympathy. This situation can be excruciatingly painful. The best outcome would be if you could face up to the 'horrors' and overcome them: things might turn out much better than you anticipate. Playing a constructive part in your team could be a good way of re-establishing your self-respect and regaining your confidence.

One of the attendant problems is that asking for a transfer will involve giving at least some explanation of why you want it, and thus telling more people – staff as well as students – about it. If you decide that the benefits of changing group outweigh the embarrassment of more people knowing about your ex-relationship, you must act quickly, because getting a transfer will usually mean exchanging with someone else, and once people have started bonding into their groups they become reluctant to move.

So have a word with the teacher in charge of allocating you to groups. Don't be surprised if he or she says they're content for you to change if *you* find someone else to change with. So be prepared to take the initiative in sounding people out. There's no need to be all 'bleeding heart' about this. Basically, you had a relationship, it didn't work out, being in the same team would be a bit awkward and distracting from the task in hand, so you'd be grateful for a swap. It needn't be a big deal.

Don't groups work best if all the members are evenly matched?

If you're one of those people who score highly in IQ tests, you may feel nervous if you find yourself in a group with others who aren't as 'IQ-clever' as you. Put those feelings to one side. Meredith Belbin describes experiments that he and colleagues carried out in the 1970s at the Administrative Staff College, Henley, in forming teams to compete in a management exercise, a game known as Teamopoly. They created one team, the 'Apollo' team, composed exclusively of members who were high-scoring on measures of mental ability. Writing about the very first time they did this, Belbin says:

> In human affairs nothing should be taken for granted. That a team of clever people should win in an exercise that placed a premium on cleverness seemed fairly obvious. [However,] the Apollo team finished last.[1]

Belbin and his colleagues carried out this experiment 25 times in total. The Apollo team won only three times. Out of eight teams competing each time, it came sixth six times and fourth four times. Good teamwork requires more than high IQs!

One of Belbin's main findings, though, has wider applicability. Essentially, it's that the most effective teams of people are those whose members' attributes are complementary. 'Even matching' implies similarity – indeed, conformity – of outlook and skills. That's fine if it means that you're all equally committed to your project; not so fine if it means you all bring to the project the same range of skills and the same way of looking at things. Variety is crucial. See Part Four, especially the section on team roles, for the different kinds of contribution you yourself can make.

To work effectively as a team member, do I have to sacrifice my individuality?

In short, no. In the prevailing UK culture, you are allowed to have your own personal goals, and it will be taken for granted that these need not be incompatible with the team's goals (as expressed, perhaps, in your mission statement). Thus, you can set your personal targets: to learn something useful and extend your portfolio of skills; to make a worthwhile contribution to the project; to enjoy your project work.

Get to know one another

Here I am with a bunch of strangers. What do I do now?

There are some academics who hold the view that, since it is a common life experience to be 'thrown in at the deep end', it will be valuable to students to have had that experience at university. Yes, you will somehow survive, but you won't appreciate being treated with such insensitivity. And sadly, since students learn by imitating their teachers as well as by studying the curriculum, some may well take a similarly insensitive attitude towards their team-mates, which is the very opposite of what good teamwork requires.

My own view is that it is not helpful to people to throw them in at the deep end without first giving them some instruction in swimming. But if that's the situation you find yourself in, it's not the end of the world.

Take the situation where you're among strangers, or fellow students whom you don't know very well. What can you do?

The first thing, of course, is to introduce yourselves to one another. Give some factual details: who you are, where you're from, what you've been doing up to now. Compare notes on courses that you've been taking and other experiences that you have had. If you're feeling a bit apprehensive about the group project, say so. Almost certainly other students will admit to the same feelings, and they will appreciate your honesty in speaking up.

Try not to be judgmental! Like most people you probably have had the experience of forming an immediate first impression of someone, perhaps based on looks or accent alone, and then revising your opinion of them as you've got to know them better. If you think back to some of your previous first meetings, you'll know that some people – perhaps you yourself are one – are quite reticent when they first meet strangers, while others – and perhaps you're one of these – are quite talkative. And you'll know too that some of the initially reticent ones open up a lot later and some of the talkative ones show that they're capable of being thoughtful and reflective. Moreover, at a first meeting we are usually more polite than we will be later, and often we're trying to impress other people. The moral: first impressions can mislead, and you don't want to be trapped by them.

A good rule in this situation, if you're among British students, is to be modest. If you're talking about your achievements, be self-deprecatory: don't boast about them, or the group may develop a competitive, 'point-scoring' atmosphere, which is not at all conducive to teamwork.

Should we try to get down to work straight away?

Probably one of the first things you should do after introducing yourselves is to go somewhere where you can talk to one another in a relaxed way. Go and have coffee or a meal together. Talk about things other than work. It's all part of creating a 'social infrastructure', a network of human relationships that will 'underpin' your project work.

Some of you may want to start taking decisions straight away: about allocating tasks – who will do what – for example. I strongly urge you not to do this. It's important that each of you first reads the assignment, your project brief (see page 41), and thinks about it before you all get together to take decisions. What you can do, though, is to sound out one another about what you are bringing to the project, in terms of both intellectual and emotional skills. But rather than ask one another 'What intellectual and emotional skills can you contribute?', you may wish to ask 'What analytical and technical skills have you got?' and 'Do you have any preferences as to the role or roles you'd like to play in the team?'. For more on team roles, see page 65.

Clearly time is a major resource we're all called upon to contribute. But I'm not sure we're all prepared to contribute the same amount, so what do we do?

You're right about seeing time as a resource. The first thing to do is to recognize the situation you're in. If, as is usually the case, you're working on your project at the same time as you're pursuing taught courses, then you'll need to make sure the project doesn't swallow up all your time, attention and energy, leaving you none for your courses. This has been known to happen! It may be worth having a discussion about what each of you thinks would be a reasonable proportion of your time to devote to the project, although some people may be more efficient users of their time and some may have more to learn. So this discussion will inevitably be somewhat hypothetical. Better perhaps to raise this issue along with that of fair division of labour when you are considering the allocation of work among you.

One of the people in my group has pointed out that our project contributes only a fraction of the mark for the course as a whole, and is questioning whether it's sensible to put in a huge amount of time and effort to getting a distinction rather than just a pass.

The strength of your motivation to do well will naturally depend on the 'incentive structure' created by the marking scheme that your teachers have designed. Ideally – to my mind – there will be enough marks for a good project outcome to make it worth spending time and effort on. And the marking scheme should also include a component based on a self- and peer-assessment, in which each member of the team assesses their own and everybody else's contribution to the work of the team. This can cover attendance at team meetings, communication and interaction with the other members of the team (including facilitating the contribution of others), contribution to the planning of the work, contribution to the leadership and management of the work of the team, and contribution to the final products.

Our project will be given a single mark, and this is the mark that each of us gets. So if the project gets a good mark, someone who has made only a small contribution will nevertheless get a good mark. It doesn't seem very fair, or calculated to get everyone to work their hardest.

The nature of group project work is such that it's often quite difficult to identify the contribution that each individual makes: one person might contribute analysis, another ideas, others writing and presentation skills, yet another may have performed the function of keeping the team united. And if individual contributions are assessed, that creates an incentive to people to work on their own contribution to the detriment of the project as a whole. A self- and peer-assessment on the lines described above should help to reward those who 'pull their weight' and penalize those who don't. Having said that, the 'free-rider' problem is a recognized one, and you'll find more about it in Part Five.

Formulate your ground rules

The value of ground rules

What do we need 'ground rules' for?

If you're in a group made up of people who haven't worked together before, you need some kind of framework to synchronize your expectations of one another, so that you are able to work smoothly together even under pressure. A set of 'ground rules' provides that framework. Ground rules can include a 'mission statement' and rules about practicalities, such as how you communicate with one other, how you arrange and conduct meetings, and how you take decisions.

Below I offer answers to questions that you may have about ground rules and their suggested components: mission statements, communications, meetings, and decision taking.

Do we need to meet to draw up our ground rules?

In theory you could work on these without meeting – one person might draft them and circulate their draft to the others – but coming up with your ground rules is a process that requires 'scenario thinking', brainstorming to imagine how you will be working together and the various situations that might arise, and this will be far more effective if you do it all together. Meeting to draw up ground rules is an opportunity – possibly your first – to do something as a collective and to get to know one another before you get down to work on the project itself. It's an opportunity you should take.

Meeting serves another purpose too. In agreeing ground rules each of you is committing himself or herself to abiding by them. You should find that collectively committing yourselves to your ground rules is a unifying, team-building act.

Mission statements

What goes in a mission statement?

A mission statement is a broad statement, expressing the 'values' that you all share. So producing it requires each of you to think about those values, and make them explicit. To get you started, here are some examples of what a mission statement could cover:

- Your aspirations (e.g. 'to produce the very best piece of work that we are capable of', 'to produce something original').
- The principles to which you all subscribe (e.g. 'to treat each other with respect', 'to acknowledge everyone's contribution').
- Individual goals which you all share (e.g. 'to learn as much as we can from the experience', 'to make good use of our skills').

A mission statement serves as a kind of flag that you rally together under. You may find that telling each other 'Remember our mission' is quite a unifying thing to do when you're having a disagreement.

Communication

Isn't communicating actually pretty straightforward?

Things can go terribly wrong if you haven't got communication sorted out between you. Imagine the situation where you've had a meeting, agreed on a set of assumptions, and gone off to work individually on your sub-tasks; then one or two people encounter a problem, see a way of getting round it that is obviously brilliant but requires changing some assumptions, and proceed enthusiastically on the basis of the changed assumptions, but unfortunately overlook the need to tell the others. It happens! And it can create a huge amount of frustration, bitterness and resentment on the part of the others when they subsequently find out.

Things can go wrong when you're using email too. Have you ever received an email that made you feel angry? That you found really offensive? Have you ever sent one that produced from the recipient a reaction that you had completely failed to anticipate? Try asking these questions when you're formulating your ground rules. When you're sending an email to someone you don't know very well, it is terribly easy to misjudge the tone. If you leave out the salutations (Hi! ... Cheers! Dear X ... Regards), the recipient may think you're being brusque if not actually rude. You may think you're being businesslike or conversational; the recipient may feel you're being high-handed. Best to err on the side of politeness, at least at first, even if you don't actually write this into your ground rules.

What ground rules about communication should we have?

Think first about the media that are available to you. There are of course face-to-face meetings, which I consider below; then there's email and phone, both landline and mobile. The latter also offer text messaging, as you doubtless know perfectly well.

Both email and phone have their 'pluses and minuses' as means of communication. You can see these in Table 1. What this table shows is that different communication media are appropriate to different situations.

Table 1: Email or phone? Pluses and minuses

Communication medium	Pluses	Minuses
Email	(1) You can send exactly the same message to everyone else (2) You can send a message at any time of day or night without disturbing the recipient (3) You can attach documents to your messages	(1) For the message to get through, you depend on the recipient to collect it (2) If the recipient's mailbox is full, your message won't be delivered (3) Unless you have arranged for your message to trigger a receipt when opened *and* you are always seated at your permanently-on computer, you won't know whether they have received it or not (4) You have no idea what impact your message is having on the recipient
Phone	(1) If you get through, (a) you know that your message has been received (b) you can judge how it has been received, match your tone to that of the recipient, and deal with any queries (2) If everyone carries a mobile, (a) using it can be an effective way of tracking someone down if they haven't shown up at a meeting, or of getting through to the others if you've been held up (b) leave them an inexpensive text message if they're out of contact	(1) You can't phone at any time (it's unwise to phone people in the middle of the night): even at other times you risk calling at an inconvenient time (not unknown between 'morning people' and 'evening people') (2) You don't have the facilities that email does of sending precisely the same message to everyone and of attaching documents (3) If you leave a text message you don't know if and when it has been read

So here are some suggestions for ground rules to do with email and phone communication:

● We shall keep in touch with all other members, especially to keep everyone abreast of progress on sub-tasks. If we're encountering problems, we shan't keep them to ourselves.

● We shall use both phone *and* email, whichever is appropriate to the needs of the moment. (Emailed circulars are best for messages about progress, because everyone is kept informed and gets the same message.) We have ensured that we all have each other's phone numbers and email addresses, and that we know if anyone doesn't have access to email where they live.

● We shall check our email and voicemail every day and keep our email-boxes clear so that all email sent to us is actually delivered.

Of course, there's more to communication than just using media for sending messages. Good communication is fundamental to teamwork, and no set of ground rules can deal with all aspects of it, but it's worth thinking even at this stage about how you *respond* to messages. You might like to have a ground rule along these lines:

● We appreciate the importance of listening to one another, acknowledging one another's work/contributions, and being constructive when giving feedback. If the occasion arises when criticism is called for, we shall make it clear that we are criticizing the work, not the person.

Meetings

Why do we need meetings? How often should we meet? And how long should our meetings be?

If your project has been genuinely designed as a task that requires teamwork, it will not be capable of being broken down into self-contained sub-tasks that can be carried out independently. Even if it does at a first glance seem capable of being so broken down, that is almost certainly a trap. So even if there are five 'deliverables' and there are five of you in your group, don't jump to the conclusion that all you have to do is to tackle one each and that you can each go off and do your own thing.

It is the interdependence of the sub-tasks making up the overall task that requires you to meet together. Meetings are of course another communication medium, face-to-face. It's worth distinguishing between informal meetings and formal, 'business' ones.

If you all bump into each other most days in lectures or classes, informal meetings will be taking place all the time. You might want to use those opportunities to chat about what you've read or been thinking, how work on sub-tasks has been going, and so on.

But keep business meetings separate, especially if not all of you meet regularly in an informal setting. (If this is the case, there's the danger that those who do often meet informally become a sub-group and that those who aren't in this sub-group feel excluded: not conducive to good teamwork.) At times when there are problems facing you, pressures upon you, and decisions to be taken, it is crucial that you deal with them when you are all present; that you have an agreed agenda; that you talk issues through, with everyone having the opportunity to participate on equal terms; that you systematically identify and assess the options open to you; and that you take and record decisions in a way that you are all content with. All this requires a degree of formality in your meeting arrangements.

As for the frequency and duration of meetings, these will depend on the stage that you're at and the issues that face you. There is no 'right' pattern. Typically meetings will be more frequent early in the process, when uncertainty is greatest; then there may be a flurry towards the end when the deadline for completion is looming and there are some hard choices to be made about reports and presentation. Duration will of course depend on how talkative and disciplined (or undisciplined) you are, as well as the number and difficulty of the items on your agenda and your tolerance of long meetings. There is usually a balance to be struck between frequency and duration: if you adopt the rule that no meeting should last longer than 90 minutes, you may find that you need to meet more frequently than if you allow a meeting to go on as long as it takes.

Do we need a chairperson? Or even a leader?

There is no one right formula for chairing meetings. Some groups like to elect a leader/chairperson. Some don't want a chairperson at all. Frequently student groups opt to have a 'rotating' chair. It feels democratic – everyone has a turn at being chairperson – and it doesn't concentrate power in the hands of one person. It also feels appropriate to the absence of 'status differentiation' among you: as students, you're all equal. And deciding to have a rotating chair, if only for the time being, avoids having a competition for the post: anyone who harbours the ambition to be chairperson will have to exercise restraint.

If you are going to have a fixed or rotating chair, you'll need to think about what the chairperson's functions (duties) will be. Two important functions are those of keeping discipline and facilitating everyone's participation. By 'keeping discipline' I mean doing things like making sure that only one person at a time speaks, and keeping discussion focused on the agenda (e.g. calling the meeting to order when the discussion is going round in circles). By 'facilitating everyone's participation' I mean making sure that everyone has an opportunity to contribute to discussion, especially people who are less vocal, less assertive, and/or less impassioned. If you have a rotating chair, the implication is that everyone will have to develop their chairing skills.

If you decide not to have a fixed or rotating chair, but to operate very much as a collective, you should consider how the 'keeping discipline' and 'facilitating everyone's participation' functions will be carried out. The implication, I think, is that everyone must take responsibility for them.

Incidentally, a useful device for aiding discipline and participation in meetings is the 'talking stick'. The idea is that only the person holding the stick – it doesn't actually need to be a stick! it could be another object, such as a book – is permitted to talk. So if you're talking and holding the 'talking stick', no one else can interrupt you. And if you want to hear what someone who has been very quiet has to say, you pass the stick to them.

As for choosing a leader, at the stage of formulating ground rules it's almost certainly too early to choose a leader for yourselves, even if you anticipate that you will be wanting to have one of you in that role. When you start work you'll be better placed to assess each other's leadership qualities.

Do we need to keep a record of everything that's said in meetings?

As regards keeping a record, you may wish to consider (a) what it is that you will want to record, and (b) whom you wish to do the recording. You will certainly want to keep a record of decisions taken: whether you do more than that (e.g. keep a record of what is said in discussions) will depend on whether you think the burden of work is outweighed by the benefits – and, of course, on whether you can find a willing volunteer. Don't underestimate the importance of the recorder's role. Not only do records of decisions taken help to ensure that you become and remain committed to acting on those decisions; the recorder who asks at indecisive moments 'Exactly what do you want me to write down?' can be wonderfully effective at getting people to focus their minds.

Should it be a normal expectation that every member attends all meetings and turns up on time?

These questions go beyond merely practical issues. Coming to meetings is not only a matter of dealing with business and making sure that everyone participates in discussion and decision making: it signifies the continuing commitment of individuals to the success of the project and their acceptance of obligations to one another. You may like to consider imposing sanctions – fines, even? – on members who are late for meetings or fail to show up without letting anyone know.

What ground rules about meetings should we have?

Here are some suggestions for ground rules to do with meetings:

- We shall meet as a team at a regular time and place, with extra meetings when necessary. At the end of each meeting, we shall confirm the time and place of the next one.
- An agenda will be drawn up in advance of each meeting. Everyone will be able to place items on the agenda and will know in advance what is to be discussed.
- We shall aim to complete business within 90 (?) minutes.
- We shall have a rotating chair for the first few meetings.
- We shall all take responsibility for keeping discipline and facilitating everyone's participation, rather than expecting the chairperson to do all

the exercising of these functions. We'll use a 'talking stick' if this becomes difficult.

- We shall take it in turns – unless there is a volunteer – to record the decisions that we take at meetings.
- It will be a normal expectation that every member attends all meetings and turns up on time.

Taking decisions

Is there a right way to take decisions?

For your decision-taking process to be effective, the decisions that you take – typically about what you are going to do, and how – must 'stick'. That's to say, once they're taken, everyone must be committed to them. So taking a decision isn't just a matter of finding the course of action that commands a majority; it's also a matter of getting the minority to accept the majority decision and not retreat into sulks or sabotage.

Ideally, then, you will seek consensus. But what if there's a major disagreement and you can't reach consensus? In that case, the advice must be to seek it so far as you can. Remember that decisions aren't instantaneous events. There is always a process leading up to them. You need to ensure that this process includes a full and frank exploration and discussion of the issue, to maximize the likelihood that those who lose out feel their point of view has had a fair hearing before the decision, and so will accept the outcome with good grace.

Bear in mind that it's sometimes possible to resolve a deadlock by reframing the issue or by extending the range of alternative courses of action you've identified. Thus, sometimes asking the question 'Do we actually need to decide this now?' will reveal that the issue can be side-stepped for the moment while more information is gathered. And asking 'Is there a course of action that combines the best points of those we've already identified?' may reveal the possibility of a compromise.

Shortly you will have decisions to take about the allocation of work. How will you take them? Will you have a bidding process, where the loudest, most assertive members grab the piece of work, the sub-task, they want? The danger is that the quietest person agrees to take on the last one left, feeling perhaps that it's their duty to do the best for the group, even though it's the last piece of work that they would want to do, and they feel they aren't knowledgeable or skilled enough to do it . . . and then struggling and getting really depressed . . . This is where you will need the skills of the chairperson, to ensure that that quiet, unassuming person is able to participate fully in the decision-taking process and isn't squeezed out. He or she may well have as much to contribute as anyone else in the group. It is, I suggest, the role of each of you to ensure that everyone has the chance to realize their full potential.

Here are some suggestions for ground rules to do with taking decisions:

- We shall seek consensus wherever possible. If necessary, we shall explore ways of reframing the issue or examining a wider range of alternatives.

- If consensus eludes us, we shall have a vote, but a vote will be taken only after everyone has had their say.

- When it comes to allocating work, we shall ensure that everyone has the same opportunity to express their preference.

Finally, here are two more suggestions for ground rules:

- We shall never let a meeting end without everyone being absolutely clear what they are to go away and do.

- We shall keep our ground rules under review. We realize that we are drawing up our original ground rules before we've started work, and that once we get into our project we may find that changes may be called for.

And when you've drawn up your ground rules, I suggest that each of you signs a master copy. Commit yourselves to them!

Check out your assignment and plan your work

The project brief

How do we actually start work?
What do we do first?

It is important that you don't start by having just a quick read of the paperwork and then dashing off in different directions.

The first thing to do is to check out your assignment. Each of you should have a paper copy of your project brief – your 'terms of reference' – and should study it carefully. (There's a lesson for life here: always read the instructions! And then read them again, because there are bound to be things whose significance you missed on your first reading!) If your teachers give you a verbal briefing, take notes as fully as you can. Making a tape recording of the verbal briefing would be a good idea.

If your assignment has been designed to provide a learning experience and has some similarity or relevance to a task you might encounter in the world of work, then (1) it will almost certainly have a challenging level of complexity; and (2) it will pose problems that are not apparent at first sight but will be revealed only as your work progresses.

So read the brief on your own and then get together with the others to pool your ideas about it and explore its implications. Here are some questions to get you started:

- Do we all understand the brief? Do we all have the same understanding? Do we agree on what is meant by any technical terms or other language whose meaning isn't immediately apparent? If not, how can we find out? Are there books, articles, manuals, websites etc. that we should consult, or people we should ask?

- Is our brief complete, i.e. sufficient in itself as a guide to what we must do? Do we have to write our own brief, in full or in part?

- Are we clear what we are expected to deliver at the conclusion of the project? In addition to 'the product', deliverables might include a literature review, and reports describing the product's form and features, evaluating and justifying it, and giving an account of the process by which you arrived at it. You might also be asked to produce a presentation for/to an audience.

- What is the purpose of the project, the object of the exercise? What skills are we expected to acquire and/or demonstrate? How shall we be assessed? Is this a test of our creativity? Our practical and literature research skills? Our technical skills? Our ability to find the right answer? (Is there one?) Our teamwork ability?

Seeking answers to these questions will get you under the skin of the project, so to speak, and save you from treating it in a superficial way.

Our project seems to be based on one encountered in the real world. But if that's the case, are we meant to treat it as something more than an academic study?

This is an important question and one that must be asked at the very beginning. It's a question about the role of your team as a whole. Let me break it into two. First, are you expected to act as students, or as practitioners or consultants? Second, who are you undertaking your project *for*? Your teacher or other members of the academic community? Your make-believe employer? A judge? A client? If the latter, would this be an individual person, a business, a governmental or non-governmental body, or – at one remove – a business's customers or shareholders, or certain sections of the public?

The answers to these questions will determine the form of your product and how you present it.

The elements of project work

What do we actually have to do to get our project going?

There is no 'one size fits all' answer to this question. Your approach will depend very much on the subject you are studying. A pure science project will necessarily involve a different set of activities from an architecture project, or one in the field of aeronautical engineering, information systems, business studies, law, or the planning of social provision. But they do have a number of kinds of activity in common, and these are shown in Box 3. Use this list to help you identify what it is that you have to do for your particular project, especially those that you will need to do to get started.

Box 3

Project activities

- *Exploration*: Investigation, experiment, discovery. Elaboration and elucidation of the brief. What questions do we need to find answers to? What issues do we have to resolve? What problems do we face?

- *Theorizing*: Viewing the task from different perspectives; expressing it in terms of concepts, hypotheses, variables and causal relationships; seeing it in context and/or as a special case of a general phenomenon or issue.

- *Data gathering*: Fieldwork, desk research, literature review; search for sources, resources and materials. What information do we need, and how can we obtain it? How have similar problems been tackled in the past?

- *Analysis*: Treatment of data, obtaining of findings, assessment of significance, inference of 'needs'; understanding how present situation came about; identification of scope for action ('area of discretion' within constraints).

- *Design*: Formulation of proposals/recommendations, including alternatives; use of techniques for deriving these from results of analysis; modelling, application of problem-solving methods; input of creativity, ingenuity, innovation, lateral thinking.

- *Evaluation*: Testing of product against requirements of brief; identifying criteria for comparing alternative proposals.

- *Presentation*: Preparation of product and other deliverables, in light of your role in relation to your audience.

Programmes of work: the 'critical path'

How should we plan our programme of work?

There are two things you need to do at the outset. One is to identify as many as you can of the *activities* that will need to be carried out; the other is to identify what will be the critical *events* in your project work. Whereas activities are carried out over a period of time, events take place at certain points in time.

Some of the forthcoming critical events you identify will be 'deadlines', i.e. points in time by which you are required to have done something. The most critical of these will of course be the day and time by which you must submit – hand in – your completed project. You may also be required to hand in a plan or report at an intermediate point. The other critical events will be decisions, points at which choices have to be made and options closed off.

Using the list of kinds of activity shown in Box 3, have a shot at breaking down your overall task – successful completion of the project – into smaller units of work, individual tasks ('sub-tasks', if you like). There can be no general rules about this: it depends on the specifics of your project. But matters are likely to be clearest around the beginning and end of your work programme. Your earliest, immediate activities will comprise the necessary preparatory work: to explore the implications of your project brief, to do any background reading required, to investigate the techniques you will (or may) have to use, and so on. Among your final activities will be work on your product: to compile and edit your final report, to create an effective presentation of your product, etc.

Once you are reasonably clear about the activities and events with which you begin and end your programme, pencil in – tentatively – some intermediate ones. For example, you may envisage at some intermediate point evaluating and then making a choice between alternative products, and you may want to allow time for commenting on a draft report.

When you first do this, it is unlikely that you will be able to foresee all the events that lie ahead and all the particular tasks that face you, especially as project work is always a learning process too, so unexpected things are liable to happen and it is sensible to build some flexibility, some 'slack', into your programme to accommodate these.

But there are some things you can and should get together and do as early as you can, once you have a picture of the events and activities that lie ahead:

- Take the largest sheet of paper you can find (or tape several sheets together). In 'landscape' orientation, draw a horizontal 'time-line', so you have a linear calendar covering the time from now to 'hand-in' day. Mark on it all deadlines and other significant events, like the completion of various stages of your work. Add further such events, as it becomes clearer what you have to do.

- Ask yourselves which events or tasks have to take place or be completed before others can take place or be completed, and which tasks can be carried out simultaneously, 'in parallel'. Pay particular attention to the sequences of tasks that cannot be carried out in parallel: that is to say, one has to be completed before the next can be undertaken. Estimate as best you can the time that each activity will take. The sequence of activities, from start to finish, that will take up the most time, is known as the 'critical path': thus the critical path determines the minimum time you will need to complete your project. During your project work you will need to keep a close eye on the activities that lie on your critical path to make sure you aren't over-running, because a delay in any of those activities will delay completion of the project. And watch out for other activities that are over-running: you may find that a different sequence is now your critical path.

● If you wish, you can develop your critical path analysis and time-line chart into more sophisticated project planning tools. You can turn your critical path analysis into a network diagram, and you can turn your time-line chart into a 'Gantt chart': a horizontal bar chart on which each activity is represented by its own horizontal bar, running from its start date to its finish date. The bars representing those activities that lie on the critical path can be joined up end to end. The Gantt chart will provide you with a picture at any given time of where you ought to be – what activities should be going on, and how close to completion they should be – and you can compare where you ought to be with where you actually are. If you use these visual aids, make it someone's responsibility to bring them to all team meetings. The development and application of critical path analysis and Gantt charts are outside the scope of this book, but you will find useful sources in 'Further reading' on page 125.

Allocating tasks

Once we've identified particular tasks, how should we go about allocating them among ourselves?

I suggest that you begin by discussing the principles on which you want to allocate tasks. Basically, there are two such principles. One is the 'expertise principle', that of making most efficient use of the expertise available to you; the other is the 'learning principle', that of maximizing the opportunities for learning for each of you.

If you adopt the expertise principle, each task would be given to the person best equipped to undertake it. Referring back to the activities listed in Box 3, you might feel that the activities of exploration, theorizing, data gathering, analysis, design, evaluation and presentation should be allocated to the member who is strongest in each. Since there almost certainly would be gaps and overlaps, you would also have to work out how to deal with these, at the same time as ensuring a fair division of labour among you all.

If you adopt the learning principle, each task could be given to the volunteer who wishes to gain experience in an activity where they feel they are currently lacking. The danger here is that the idealism inherent in this approach is overcome by the pressure to produce the best possible product: there is unlikely to be time for much trial and error and reflection, and likely to be increasing impatience with the slowest learners.

There is, however, a middle approach, which has a great deal to commend it: that you work in pairs, each task being tackled by an expert and a learner working together. I have known this to work well.

I have also known a group who discovered early on that each of them thought they knew best how to proceed and were unwilling to delegate tasks to anyone else. They got round this by deciding they would do everything together. The ferocity of their arguments amazed all who witnessed it, but by the end of the project they had bonded into a team of remarkable unity.

Finally, please avoid allocating tasks through a process of bidding in which the most assertive person gets what they want. See the warning under 'Taking decisions' in the section 'Formulate your ground rules' above.

Part Three

How are we doing?

The question 'How are we doing?' can be asked in relation to the task, to the team as a whole, and to individuals. Discussion of all of these, on an occasion where you take time out away from the project, can reveal issues that haven't surfaced up to now, allow them to be discussed in a non-blaming way – this is crucial! – and yield valuable 'action points' for getting back on track to completing your project in line with your mission statement.

Progress on the project

How should we monitor our progress on our project?

It is crucial to monitor the progress you are making both with your overall task and the individual tasks that members are carrying out. If you get behind with the overall task, you won't have enough time to do a good job in the later stages. So check progress regularly against your time-line chart and critical path, not forgetting to update these as it becomes clearer what you will have to do to complete the project.

How can we be sure that everyone is getting on with the tasks allocated to them?

In many student teams this becomes a crucial question. It is in the nature of academic project work that people take their tasks away from meetings, work on them by themselves, and then come back to the team with their results. If someone doesn't show up to meetings and 'goes quiet', both the non-delivery of results and the uncertainty as to what's going on can be very hard on the other members.

There are two things you can do to try to prevent this situation arising. One is to allocate work to pairs of people rather than individuals (another reason for putting an expert and a learner together). The other is to have regular team meetings – once a week will usually be appropriate – at which the first substantive item on the agenda is always reports on progress from everybody, i.e. reports on what you have all done since the last meeting. You could write this into your ground rules. An extra benefit of doing this is that it very quickly becomes apparent if people are working on different assumptions or if someone has misunderstood what they were supposed to be doing. And sometimes people take it into their heads to 'strike out on their own': insisting on regular reporting is a way of keeping the team together.

It feels like for every two steps forward, we're taking one step back. Is this normal?

It *is* normal to get this feeling at some point during a project. It comes about because some of your project activities – especially exploration, design and presentation – are 'trial-and-error' ones, so there are bound to be some 'errors'. If you think of the project as a learning process, and bear in mind that you are learning even from errors, it may be some consolation that even a step back takes you forward in your learning.

It follows that you should always be prepared to write off work when it has become apparent that it's not going to be fruitful. One of the problems with project work is that people become so committed to ideas and proposals, by virtue of the effort they've invested in them, that they are very reluctant to take that step back. Mature teamworkers recognize this situation and accept some writing off as unavoidable.

No sooner do we deal with one problem than we find ourselves facing another one. Is this inevitable?

This happens in all project work, I believe. It can come about because you're progressively getting into finer and finer detail, progressing from a broad outline or general principles to a fully specified product. Decisions have to be taken at all levels. It can also come about by virtue of the inter-connectedness of various features of your product and the other deliverables: if everything is connected to everything else, then a decision taken on one feature has repercussions for all the others.

Progress from 'group' to 'team'

In Box 4 you'll find an 'Are we a team?' questionnaire. This has been designed to help you assess the extent to which you have become a team rather than a group. I suggest that you make a photocopy of the questionnaire for each of you, that you each fill it in on your own, without discussion, and that you then put your scores together, using the scoresheet in Box 5. See which are the two criteria with the lowest scores, and then take some time for each of you to explain to one another why you have given them a low score. Then formulate two 'action points', things you can do to improve matters on those two criteria.

Box 4

Are we a team? Questionnaire

Make a photocopy of the questionnaire below. Then, working on your own, without conferring with your team-mates, score your team on each of the following statements. Write down your score after each statement, taking

1 = never; 2 = rarely; 3 = sometimes; 4 = mostly; 5 = always.

(1) We all show equal commitment to our objective . . . . . .

(2) We all take part in deciding how work should be allocated . . . . . .

(3) We are committed to helping each other learn . . . . . .

(4) We acknowledge good contributions from team members . . . . . .

(5) We handle disagreements and conflicts constructively within the team . . . . . .

(6) We are able to give constructive criticism to one another and to accept it . . . . . .

(7) We all turn up to meetings and stay to the end . . . . . .

(8) We are good at making sure that everyone knows what's going on . . . . . .

(9) When one of us is under pressure, others offer to help them . . . . . .

(10) We trust each other . . . . . .

(11) We remain united even when we disagree . . . . . .

(12) We feel comfortable and relaxed with one another . . . . . .

(13) We refer to our ground rules and review them when necessary . . . . . .

(With acknowledgements to Roderick Stuart, *Team Development Games for Trainers* (Gower 1998), and http://www.teambuilding.co.uk/behaviours.htm)

Box 5

Are we a team? Scoresheet

Enter in the respective columns the scores that each of you individually gave your team on each criterion. Then add the scores for each criterion (i.e. in each row) and enter them in the TOTAL column.

	1	2	3	4	5	TOTAL
(1) We all show equal commitment to our objective						
(2) We all take part in deciding how work should be allocated						
(3) We are committed to helping each other learn						
(4) We acknowledge good contributions from team members						
(5) We handle disagreements and conflicts constructively within the team						
(6) We are able to give constructive criticism to one another and to accept it						
(7) We all turn up to meetings and stay to the end						
(8) We are good at making sure that everyone knows what's going on						
(9) When one of us is under pressure, others offer to help them						
(10) We trust each other						
(11) We remain united even when we disagree						

	1	2	3	4	5	TOTAL
(12) We feel comfortable and relaxed with one another						
(13) We refer to our ground rules and review them when necessary						

Personal progress

Working in a team on a project can be both stressful and rewarding. So you may find yourself experiencing a wide range of feelings, possibly fluctuating from day to day. Meeting together to do the 'Are we a team?' exercise will provide an opportunity to express and share your feelings, but some or all members may feel that the prime purpose of meetings is to progress the project, not to provide therapy.

In Box 6 you'll find a short 'How am I doing?' questionnaire. This has been designed to help you individually assess the extent to which you have begun to realize your personal goals and are coping with the stresses of teamwork. The questions are designed primarily to get you thinking, and because it's an individual matter there's no need for scoring. For suggestions as to what you might do to improve matters, see the sections on individual issues in Part Five.

Box 6

How am I doing? Questionnaire

(1) How is my work for the project going?

(2) What aspects of the project do I feel good about? (Are my personal goals being met? Am I making a worthwhile contribution to the project? Am I learning something useful?)

(3) What aspects of the project do I have negative feelings about?

(4) How good are my relationships with each other member of the team?

(5) What can I do to maintain the good things about the project, to improve the less good ones, and – if called for – to improve my relationships with other members?

Part Four

Perspectives on team behaviour

How can you stand back from the hurly-burly of teamwork and make sense of what is going on in your team? In the following sections I introduce a variety of perspectives on team dynamics. You can use them in two ways.

First, you can use the perspectives to gain an explanation of what's going on in your team, of the behaviour that you have observed. This isn't just an intellectual exercise: it can be very reassuring to discover that seemingly irrational behaviour does in fact have a good explanation.

Second, you can use these perspectives to work out strategies for dealing with issues and improving your team's performance. For example, they can help in resolving conflicts, making better use of everyone's aptitudes, and finding a way forward when some necessary work isn't getting done.

Incidentally, you can also test the perspectives against your own experience, which will help you to develop a critical approach to the literature, rather than to take it as gospel.

Tensions: the task, the team and the individual

John Adair, in his book *Effective Teambuilding: How to Make a Winning Team*, identifies three distinct needs as being 'present in the life of every group'.[2] Slightly adapting his framework, we can distinguish between:

- the needs – the demands – of the task, i.e. the requirement that the project be successfully undertaken;
- the needs of the team, the need to develop and maintain working relationships among the members so that the team task can be accomplished;
- the needs of the individuals who make up the team.

As you can see, I have already adopted this three-way distinction in the previous three sections of this book (Progress on the project; Progress from 'group' to 'team'; Personal progress).

Adair argues that if the needs of individuals can be met along with and not at the expense of the demands of the task and the needs of the team, then the team will tend to be more effective than it otherwise would be.

My own take on this is somewhat different. It is this:

● Overall, a balance requires to be kept between the needs of the task, the needs of the team, and the needs of individual team members.

At different points in the process, there may be pressure for needs of one kind or another to take precedence over others. For example, at the beginning some members may feel it urgent to give priority to bonding, i.e. to the needs of the team, and work on the project is slow to get off the ground. Around the mid-point you may find a member who has a psychological need to get his or her own way exerting pressure on the others and causing dissent and disharmony within the team. Towards the deadline for hand-in the need to complete the project will inevitably predominate over all others, and those taking the lead at this point may sometimes be found riding roughshod over the feelings of the others and careless of the impact on the 'togetherness' of the team.

It follows that you can explain – make sense of – some kinds of team behaviour by examining where the balance is currently lying between task needs, team needs, and the needs of individuals. And you can often find a remedy for 'dysfunctional' behaviour by looking for ways of restoring the balance.

There is one important qualification to the three-fold distinction between task, team and individual needs. It sometimes happens that sub-groups, cliques and alliances form, and these begin to assert their own needs: for power and control, for example. If such sub-groups have come about, then you're looking at four sets of needs, and you have to examine a four-way balance.

Team roles

Today the best-known writer on the subject of work teams and team roles is probably Meredith Belbin, who for nearly a decade worked with (and experimented on) managers attending courses at the Administrative Staff College, Henley. The thesis of Belbin's book *Management Teams: Why They Succeed or Fail*, first published in 1981 and still in print, and his later book, *Team Roles at Work*,[3] is based on two underlying premises: that people placed in a team tend to carve out a role for themselves that suits their personal preferences and predilections, and that for a complex task to be carried out successfully by a team of people, all team roles need to be played.

In both his books Belbin identifies archetypal 'team roles'. Initially there were eight of these: he later added a ninth (specialist). Somewhat confusingly, these are a mixture of behaviours (both general and specific), aims, and personal traits. Table 2 – compiled by trawling through both books – summarizes these.

Table 2: Belbin's 'team roles'

1 Chairman (subsequently Co-ordinator)   A leadership role. Recognizes where the team's strengths and weaknesses lie, and ensures that the best use is made of each team member's potential. Makes interventions that are most apparent at critical points, striving 'to pull the whole thing together'. Never allows meetings to get out of hand, and at moments of dissension is ready to impart a sense of direction and purpose. Is able to control team members effectively. Acts as a unifier in the pursuit of common objectives. Mature, confident, a good chairperson. **But** can be seen as manipulative; delegates personal work.
2 Shaper   Also a leadership role. Shapes the way in which team effort is applied, directs attention generally to the setting of objectives and priorities, and seeks to impose some shape or pattern on group discussion and on the outcome of group activities. Abounds in nervous energy, actuated by the need for achievement, impatient and easily frustrated. Prone to challenge, argue, disagree, create uproar. Leads a group in a driving, action-based, directive way, galvanizing it into action. Challenging, dynamic, thrives on pressure. Has the drive and courage to overcome obstacles. **But** can provoke others. Hurts people's feelings.
3 Plant   Advances new ideas and strategies with special attention to major issues, and looks for possible breaks in approach to the problems with which the group is confronted. Creative, innovative, original, a wayward genius. Liable to sit in a corner on his or her own, thinking things through and sometimes coming up with some winning possibility. Has strategic ability. Essentially introverted, very clever. Creative, imaginative, unorthodox. Solves difficult problems. **But** ignores details. Too preoccupied to communicate effectively. (Belbin named this role 'plant' because he planted such individuals into groups for experimental purposes.)
4 Resource investigator   Explores and reports on ideas, developments and resources outside the group, creating external contacts that may be useful to the team and conducting any subsequent

negotiations. Creative by virtue of close involvement with other people and skill in using resources. Resourceful in making the most of interpersonal opportunities, ensures no stone left unturned in search for ideas. Has innovative opportunism and presence/ quickness of mind. Uninhibited about finding out what he or she wants to know by making good use of other people. Gets around, finds out what is going on, meets people, poses well-thought-out questions. Has the knack of doing business and also of getting new things started. Outgoing, extroverted, inquisitive. Extrovert, enthusiastic, communicative. **But** over-optimistic. Loses interest once initial enthusiasm has passed.

5 Monitor–evaluator

Analyses problems and evaluates ideas and suggestions so that the team is better placed to take balanced decisions. Suited to the task of sorting out the best ideas. Can hold his or her own in debate with a Plant. Slow in coming to a judgment, prefers to think things over. Not swayed by emotionally loaded material. Serious-minded, prudent, with a built-in immunity from enthusiasm. Judgments shrewd, taking all factors into account. Not committed to one particular course of action. Makes no claim to originality or imagination. Sober, strategic and discerning. Sees all options. Judges accurately. **But** lacks drive and ability to inspire others. Overly critical.

6 Company worker (subsequently Implementer)

Turns concepts and plans into practical working procedures, and carries out agreed plans systematically and efficiently. Essentially works for the team or company, rather than in pursuit of self-interest, and does so in a practical and realistic way. Will get on with the jobs that need doing even though they may be far from intrinsically interesting or pleasant. Disciplined, reliable, conservative and efficient. **But** somewhat inflexible. Slow to respond to new possibilities.

7 Completer–finisher (subsequently just Completer)

Ensures that the team is protected as far as possible from mistakes of both commission and omission, actively searches for aspects of work which need a more than usual degree of attention, and maintains a sense of urgency within the team. Has the ability to finalize whatever is started and to do so with thoroughness. Plans ahead, gives attention to detail and has a capacity for relentless follow-through. Is prepared to hold things back until all the necessary tests, checks and safeguards have been completed and the product can be announced as truly ready to go. Painstaking, conscientious, anxious. Searches out errors and omissions. Delivers on time. **But** inclined to worry unduly. Reluctant to delegate. Can be a nit-picker.

---

8 Team worker

Supports members in their strengths (e.g. building on suggestions), underpins members in their shortcomings, improves communications between members and fosters team spirit generally. At a tense moment may save the day with a helpful intervention that averts potential friction and enables difficult characters in the team to use their skills to positive ends. Skilled in listening to others and coping with awkward people, willing to place team objectives above self-interest. Cooperative, mild, perceptive and diplomatic. Listens, builds, calms the waters. **But** indecisive in crunch situations. Can be easily influenced.

9 Specialist

Single-minded, self-starting, dedicated. Provides knowledge and skills in rare supply. **But** contributes on only a narrow front. Dwells on technicalities. Overlooks the 'big picture'.

In *Management Teams* Belbin offers a questionnaire-based 'self-perception inventory'. If you fill in the questionnaire and the accompanying analysis sheet, you can score yourself on the first eight team roles. The team role with the highest score is the one in which, according to Belbin, you can best 'make [your] mark in a management or project team. The next highest scores can denote back-up team roles towards which [you] should shift if for some reason there is less group need for a primary team role'.[4] It can be very illuminating if everyone in your team does this exercise and you look at the results together. As a simple alternative, you and your team-mates should individually read through the outlines above and pick the two that you think best apply to you, then identify the one that is more applicable. What can you do with the results? Read on.

Belbin's framework can be used in two ways: for explanation, and for resolving issues.

Explanation: The behaviour of a team (and its success or failure in achieving its objectives) and of individual members can sometimes be explained by the existence of overlaps, gaps and 'fit' (complementarity) among the roles of individual members. For example, a team that contains a number of shapers may spend all its time arguing; a team with no chairman, shaper or monitor–evaluator may be indecisive; a team with no plant or resource investigator may not be producing ideas; and a team with no completer–finisher may fail to complete its task. Likewise the secret of a team's success may be that it has one member playing each role.

Resolving issues: If there are overlaps, it may be necessary for your team to take some decisions about the division of labour among the two or more of a kind. Or you may need to set up a formal procedure for resolving conflicts and generally taking decisions, so – for example – you choose between alternatives by comparing them on agreed criteria (rather than on the basis of who is more effective at behind-the-scenes lobbying). If there are gaps, then discuss how you could fill these: perhaps by one of you rising to the occasion and extending his or her own repertoire of aptitudes; or by two or more of you taking this role on; or by adopting a procedure that would help, such as putting on your agenda for weekly meetings the item 'What shall we need to do to complete and finish the project?' if there isn't a completer–finisher among you.

In my experience, this can be a very illuminating exercise for teams. However, I feel I must issue a 'health warning'. Although it is clear from the self-perception inventory that Belbin regards individuals as having a 'profile' of role preferences, he also refers to the eight team-roles as 'types' and describes them as 'useful people to have in teams'.[5] And the descriptions can easily be taken as labels that attach to people rather than functions. Consequently people who complete the questionnaire tend to end up thinking 'I'm a company worker/shaper ...' and as a corollary 'I'm no good as a chairman, completer–finisher ...'

Do not do this! Do not label yourself. If this is the first time you have completed the Belbin questionnaire please be aware that other people who have completed it more than once have found that they did not get the same result each time. Try this experiment. Fill in the questionnaire with a particular team experience that you've had in mind. Then fill it in with another past collective experience in mind, not necessarily to do with work: it could have been to do with a leisure activity, perhaps, or a family holiday. If you get a different profile – and especially if your highest score this time is for a different team role – you have some flexibility, and in particular some capacity to respond to a new team situation by developing a team role other than one to which you are accustomed.

Studies of team roles go back many years. Back in 1948 Kenneth D. Benne and Paul Sheats developed an analysis of the 'functional roles of group members'. Interestingly, they divided these into three groups: 'group task roles', 'group building and maintenance roles', and 'individual roles': the task/team/individual split again.[6] I have summarized these in Table 3.

Table 3: Benne and Sheats' 'functional roles'

Group task roles

Initiator–contributor suggests new ideas and ways of looking at problems or goals.

Information seeker asks for clarification and for supporting facts and authority.

Opinion seeker asks for clarification of pertinent values.

Information giver offers 'authoritative' facts or generalizations or relates relevant aspects of his or her own experience.

Opinion giver states belief or opinion, emphasizing values rather than facts or information.

Elaborator spells out suggestions (e.g. with examples), offers a rationale for proposals, and explores likely implications of proposals if adopted.

Coordinator shows or clarifies relationships among ideas and suggestions, tries to pull them together, tries to coordinate activities.

Orienter defines the group's position with respect to its goals by summarizing what has occurred, identifies departures from agreed directions or goals, or raises questions about the direction discussion is taking.

Evaluator–critic assesses suggestions, etc. and questions their practicality, their logic, the facts, the procedure, etc.

Energizer prods the group to decision, action, 'higher quality', etc.

Procedural technician expedites 'group movement' by performing routine tasks, etc.

Recorder writes down suggestions, records group decisions, etc. Acts as the 'group memory'.

Group building and maintenance roles

Encourager praises, commends, agrees with and accepts the contributions of others. Conveys warmth and solidarity.

Harmonizer attempts to reconcile disagreements, relieve tension by joking, etc.

Compromiser deals with a conflict involving his or her idea or position by giving way, admitting error, etc.

Gatekeeper and expediter attempts to keep communication channels open by encouraging or facilitating the participation of others.

Standard setter sets standards for the functioning of the group: these can be used to evaluate the quality of group processes.

Group observer and *commentator* records various aspects of group process, feeds such data and interpretations of it into the group's evaluation of its own procedures.

Follower more or less passively accepts the ideas of others, acts as an audience in group discussion and decision.

'Individual' roles

Aggressor may seek to deflate the status of others, express disapproval of the values, acts and feelings of others, joke aggressively, try to take credit for another's contribution, etc.

Blocker tends to be negative and stubbornly resistant, to disagree and oppose without or beyond 'reason', to reopen issues after the group has dealt with them.

Recognition seeker seeks to call attention to himself or herself, e.g. by boasting, reporting on personal achievements, exhibiting unusual behaviour, struggling to resist being placed in an 'inferior' position.

Self-confessor treats the group as an audience for his or her personal expressions of 'feeling', 'insight', 'ideology', etc.

Playboy makes a display of lack of involvement in the group's processes, e.g. by expressing cynicism or nonchalance, or by fooling around ('horseplay').

Dominator tries to assert authority or superiority by manipulating the group or some members; may use flattery, give directions in an authoritative manner, interrupt others when they're speaking, etc.

Help seeker attempts to elicit 'sympathy' from others, e.g. by expressing insecurity or confusion, or by being self-deprecating.

Special interest pleader claims to speak for an outside constituency, usually cloaking his or her own prejudices or biases in the stereotype which best fits their individual need.

Benne and Sheats say nothing about how they arrived at their list, but it is valuable in two ways. First, you can use it to identify the kinds of behaviour on the part of members of your team and hence gaps and undesirable behaviour that needs attention. Recognizing someone's behaviour as that of a playboy is the first step towards dealing with it.

Second, this list raises the question of what Belbin's list looks like if we try to distinguish between task, team and individual roles. In my judgment – but check this for yourself – only two of Belbin's roles, Chairman and Teamworker, are team roles as distinct from task roles and individual roles. Benne and Sheats' group building and maintenance roles – Encourager, Harmonizer, and so on – hardly feature in Belbin's list. Which, if I may be permitted a sweeping generalization, seems entirely consistent with the abysmal state of management in businesses and public sector organizations in the UK today.

Finally, having observed some hundreds of teams at work, I'd like to offer my own list of the team roles – i.e. team-building and maintenance roles, rather than task or individual roles – which are prerequisites for well-functioning teams:

- *Organizer*: Keeps meetings focused and in order, does his or her best to get through the agenda.
- *Encourager*: Brings good-humoured appreciation to proceedings, able to defuse tensions and revive flagging morale.
- *Facilitator*: Ensures that the quieter members of the group are heard and everyone's contribution acknowledged.
- *Recorder*: Keeps a note of decisions (especially decisions as to who will do what before the next meeting), ensures that everyone is aware of them.

- *Time-keeper and progress-chaser*: Keeps an eye on the calendar and ensures that everyone is aware of the 'state of play'.
- *Coordinator*: Sees the 'big picture' (the strategic overview), with an eye for gaps and overlaps, and presents this to the team.
- *Lookout*: Visualizes future scenarios, is alert to issues that may be looming over the horizon, keeps everyone informed.

Management systems and team organization

In their classic book *The Management of Innovation*, Tom Burns and G.M. Stalker reported on 20 case studies of 'what happens when new and unfamiliar tasks are put upon industrial concerns organized for relatively stable conditions'.[7] They discovered two contrasting patterns of management system, which they termed the 'mechanistic' and the 'organic'. They argued that a mechanistic system is appropriate to stable conditions, whereas an organic system is appropriate to changing conditions, which give rise constantly to fresh problems and unforeseen requirements for action. The salient characteristics of the two kinds of system are shown in Table 4, which is slightly adapted from their original version.[8]

Table 4: Burns and Stalker: Mechanistic and organic management systems

Characteristic	Mechanistic systems	Organic systems
The nature of the organization's overall task	Can be broken down into specialized functional tasks distributed automatically within the organization	Requires the contribution of special knowledge and experience from all parts of the organization
How individual tasks are tackled	Independently of others and of the overall task	With an appreciation of the overall task facing the organization
Structure of control, authority and communication	Hierarchic structure	Network structure
How individual tasks are assigned	Tasks assigned (and products reconciled) by one's superior, i.e. at the level above	Tasks adjusted and continually redefined through interaction with others
Locus of rights, duties and methods	Rights, duties and methods specified precisely and exclusively for each position	Rights, duties and methods are collective. 'Problems may not be posted upwards, downwards or sideways as being someone else's responsibility'
Commitment expected	To doing one's own job to the best of one's ability. Loyalty to the organization and obedience to superiors required	To the organization. Commitment to its tasks and ethos particularly valued
Locus of knowledge and decision making	Information flows to the top, where decisions are made. The head of the organization is regarded as omniscient	Knowledge about the here-and-now task may be located anywhere in the network, this location becoming the ad hoc centre of control, authority and communication

Pattern of communication	Communication tends to be vertical, i.e. between superior and subordinate	Communication tends to be lateral. Between people of different rank it resembles consultation rather than command
Content of communication	Primarily instructions and decisions	Primarily information and advice

The corollary of Burns and Stalker's thesis is that if your project is one that constantly challenges you with fresh problems and unforeseen requirements for action, you should organize yourselves on the model of the organic system, as a network rather than a hierarchy.

There is, however, a difficulty with this prescription. Many people react to situations of uncertainty by seeking definiteness. They want to know where they stand. So they bid for a 'position' within the team. They seek to carve out a task for themselves over which they have full control, and resist other people's attempts to interfere (as they see it). They propose to their team-mates that the team appoint a leader, to whom they will report and whom they expect to give instructions. In other words, they attempt to force the structure into a hierarchical mould, on the mechanistic model.

Thus, if your team does not appear to be functioning well, the explanation may lie in some members acting in a 'mechanistic' rather than an 'organic' way. What can you do about this? The first thing, I think, is to recognize that hierarchies do fulfil certain basic human needs, especially for security. You do know where you stand. You have a rank, and the length of time you have occupied that rank establishes your position relative to others of the same rank. If your need for security, and that of your team-mates, is not being met by the organizational structure, it has to be met in other ways. This is a 'team need': a need for team-building and maintenance. Ideally, it will be met by all of you taking on the roles of facilitator and encourager for one another.

Team development: forming, storming, norming, performing...

In the mid-1960s, Bruce Tuckman reviewed 50 or 55 published articles reporting on studies of the development of groups of various kinds: therapy groups, human relations training groups and 'laboratory' groups, as well as 'natural' groups set up to do a job of work.[9] Tuckman drew a distinction between the 'social realm', embracing social/interpersonal group activities, and the 'task' realm, embracing task-related activities. He proposed a four-stage 'developmental model' – forming, storming, norming and performing – that applied to all groups: each stage included activities in both realms. Subsequently he and Mary Ann Jensen reviewed a further 22 studies and concluded that a further stage, adjourning, should be added.[10] The stages are summarized in Table 5.

Table 5: Tuckman's stages of group development

1 Forming
In this initial stage everyone is still orienting themselves, getting their bearings. They are finding out about one another and about the task, and a certain amount of testing goes on, in both the interpersonal realm and the task realm. Dependency relationships become established, both among group members and between group members and leaders, as a way of overcoming uncertainty and insecurity.
2 Storming
This stage, which may be brief or lengthy, is characterized by conflict and polarization around interpersonal issues. These have repercussions in the task realm. There is resistance to pressure to fit in to the group and to the demands of the task. Progress is threatened.
3 Norming
In this stage, cohesion appears among members. In the interpersonal realm, the group 'gels' into a team. Ways of working together evolve, and people may find themselves adopting new roles. In the task realm, members find that they are able to express their opinions frankly. They have a sense of pulling together, and are more sensitive to one another.
4 Performing
This is the stage in which the interpersonal structure becomes adapted to – and hence supportive of – task performance. Interpersonal problems and structural issues have been resolved. Roles have become flexible and functional, and group energy is channelled into the task.
5 Adjourning
This is the stage of 'termination', where issues relating to the break-up of the group arise and are dealt with.

The underlying premise here is evidently that progression through these five stages is in some sense 'natural', and thus inevitable. (In his original article, Tuckman drew a parallel between the first four stages and the stages through which a child develops, from infancy to maturity.) Thus, if you find yourselves 'storming', the explanation is not that there is something wrong with you, but that it is a 'natural' stage between forming and norming: members of teams where all is not running smoothly often find it reassuring to discover this.

It's worth noting too that the Tuckman model allows for some repetition, going back to an earlier stage and then moving forward again. On this view, the process can be a reiterative, cyclical one, taking you in a loop through storming, norming and performing stages. If this happens to you, again, you can be reassured that it is perfectly normal.

The decision-making process

The central point I want to make in this section is that the process of undertaking a project, from start to completion, is a process of increasing commitment to an increasingly specific product. At the point when you are about to hand it in, you are fully committed to handing in a fully specified product. And when you do hand it in, your commitment is realized, turned into action. That product incorporates the results of many decisions, and it requires little imagination to view the process as a whole as a decision-making one. But a significant ingredient of the process is the commitment that is created. Decisions create commitment, but commitment comes about in other ways too. In Table 6 are shown some of the ways in which you may find commitment coming about: (1) Taking a decision; (2) Making up your mind; (3) Investing effort; and (4) Using up time.

Table 6: The creation of commitment

Taking a decision
The taking of a decision (an event, as opposed to the process that is the *making* of a decision) can be defined as an act of conscious choice that creates commitment to one course of action rather than others. To go back on that decision and pursue a different course of action involves paying a penalty of some kind, for an individual team member or for the team as a whole. Your self-esteem suffers – e.g. you feel stupid – and the image you present to other people is likely to be dented, especially if you have argued strongly for the course of action you now have to give up.
Making up your mind
This is like a private decision. You become personally attached to your envisaged course of action: you set your heart on it, you become mentally wedded to it, and you close your mind to alternatives. Even if other people are unaware of it, severing that attachment is likely to be painful.
Investing effort
The more effort, the more time and energy, that you invest in following up one course of action – an idea or proposal, say – the more painful it becomes to relinquish it, even if an objectively better course of action is discovered. If one of your team-mates has gone into hiding for two weeks, worked tremendously hard on an aspect of your product, then emerges and proudly presents you with something that the rest of you take an instant dislike to, you will find it extremely difficult to reject it without hurting his or her feelings. They might indeed have thought about this and be banking on precisely that effect.
Using up time
If you spend 90 per cent of your time following up one particular line for your product, you have simply not left enough time to switch to a different one, even if you discover late in the day that that particular line has major drawbacks. Again, this is something that an unscrupulous team member might take advantage of. The person who is editing your final report may delete material that you feel strongly should be included, but if you discover the deletions only at the very last minute there will be no opportunity to restore them.

So the formation of commitment, in ways that are not apparent as well as in ways that are, can go a long way to explaining how you have come to get stuck with a course of action that, on reflection, you are not happy with.[11]

What can you do to prevent this happening? Here are some suggestions:

- Don't take a decision until you're sure you have enough information to be reasonably confident that you won't need to backtrack and until you have ascertained every team member's feelings about it. If you aren't as confident as you would like to be, do your best to keep some options open, even if this means pursuing two or three alternatives simultaneously for a time.

- In your own mind, don't jump to conclusions. Control your enthusiasm. Share your thoughts and ideas with your team members, rather than rushing off on your own.

- Watch out for signs that someone is investing a great deal of time and effort without reporting back to the team. (And don't do this yourself!) Make it clear that you refuse to be 'bounced' into accepting proposals that someone else has been developing without the team's authority.

- Keep your eyes on the calendar. Insist on building into your programme some 'slack' so you can review and redo work if necessary without overshooting your deadline.

Negotiation

In any project team, once it gets past the forming stage, disputes will inevitably arise. People disagree on substantive issues – to do with the shape and form, etc., of the products – and on process issues – to do with procedure: how decisions will be taken, etc. To resolve these disagreements without creating ill-will and fracturing the team, negotiation will be needed.

The classic and best-selling book on this subject, and one relevant to teamwork despite not being addressed directly to that subject, is the second edition of *Getting to Yes: Negotiating an Agreement Without Giving In*, by Roger Fisher and William Ury.[12] Fisher and Ury begin by demonstrating the danger and futility of being drawn into bargaining with someone who sets out his or her position – their demand – whether you respond in kind, by setting out your own demand, or by making offers and concessions in the hope that you can avoid confrontation. They offer a very practical approach to negotiating that is based on four principles: (1) Separate the people from the problem; (2) Focus on interests, not positions; (3) Invent options for mutual gain; and (4) Insist on using objective criteria. In Table 7 I have outlined their principles and some of their recommendations, with some interpretation of my own in order to bring out their applicability to disputes of the kind that can arise within a team.

Table 7: Fisher and Ury's negotiating principles applied to a team context

Separate the people from the problem

'The relationship tends to become entangled with the problem.' You may make what you regard as a factual statement about an issue, but the person you make it to may hear it as an attack. And from your statements and behaviour he or she may draw inferences about your attitudes towards them that are completely wrong. So you must address the relationship. Consider perceptions, emotions and communication.

Perceptions: Put yourself in their shoes, and discuss your and their perceptions. If they regard something as important, treat it as important: don't brush it aside. You may be able to change their perception of you by doing something that they don't expect you to do. Make sure they participate in the process, rather than taking decisions on their behalf, so they see themselves as having a stake in the outcome. Make suggestions that they see as consistent with principles they subscribe to, not as defeats.

Emotions: Notice your own and the other person's emotions: are you and/or they angry, fearful, anxious? It's legitimate to have feelings: invite them to say how they're feeling, and do the same yourself. Allow them to 'let off steam', and don't react to emotional outbursts. 'Freed from the burden of unexpressed emotions, people will become more likely to work on the problem.'

Communication: Listen actively and acknowledge what is being said. Find a common language, to be sure that you understand each other. Don't impute blame or fault to the other person: simply say how you feel and see matters. There's no need to say everything in your mind: don't say things that will confuse rather than clarify.

Focus on interests, not positions

To reach a 'wise' solution, aim at reconciling underlying interests, not stated demands. You have an interest in an outcome if you stand to gain or lose from it in some way, so you are motivated by your interests. Behind your stated demands, you may have more common interests than you think. Aim to get your and their interests out in the open. These interests might include security, autonomy, having their contribution acknowledged, and having a sense of belonging to the team, as well as in seeing the project successfully completed. Summarize the interests at stake, then present your proposals as an appropriate response to them, rather than stating your proposals first then citing interests to back them up. And, as Fisher and Ury put it, 'Attack the problem without attacking the people.'

Invent options for mutual gain

In many cases, the resolution of a dispute is hampered by the fact that very few solutions have been identified. A choice between 'my way' and 'your way' is not susceptible to constructive negotiation, and somebody is going to end up defeated and unhappy. To generate as many alternative solutions as possible:

- *Suspend judgment until you've brainstormed.* Fisher and Ury suggest holding brainstorming sessions in an informal environment – preferably somewhere where you don't regularly meet – and calling in a facilitator if one is available. Have a flipchart, and all sit facing it, so protagonists aren't eyeballing each other. The purpose of brainstorming is to get everyone to come up with ideas, so the rule is: no criticism during brainstorming! Once there's a list of ideas on the flipchart, star those that seem most worthwhile taking forward, then think about ways of making them more attractive. Only then get down to exercising judgment and making your final choice.

- *Broaden your options.* This is more of a reasoning process than brainstorming is. Diagnose the 'causes' of the problem: ask what combination of factors has brought it about, how some or all of these factors might be changed, what solutions others have found to similar problems, and so on.

- *Don't assume you're in a zero-sum game, where one person's win can only be achieved if another loses.* The size of the 'cake' is not necessarily fixed. An issue can be extended, broken down or combined with another. Identify goals that you share or that are complementary. People have different interests, beliefs, priorities and attitudes towards risk, so it may be possible to find an aggregate of decisions that does indeed satisfy everyone.

- *Try to make the other person's decision easy.* For example, to paraphrase Fisher and Ury, it is usually easier to persuade someone not to start doing something than to stop them once they have started. In other words, get in early, before they are committed. And it's usually easier to persuade them to do something that is consistent with their previous actions than something that isn't.

Insist on using objective criteria

If your dispute becomes a battle of wills, it can be resolved only by one side backing down under pressure. This will not be conducive to harmony in your team! So it's a task for everyone, having identified feasible alternatives and their respective likely outcomes, to think about and put forward objective criteria for assessing these outcomes. This will make the choice an objective one. Getting everyone involved in doing this will avoid the situation where one person can produce two alternatives but make one of them so unappealing that you effectively have no choice but to select the other.

In the second edition of their book, Fisher and Ury address a number of questions, including 'What do I do if the people *are* the problem?' They make four recommendations:

- *Build a working relationship that is independent of agreement or disagreement.* 'The more seriously you disagree with someone, the more important it is that you are able to deal well with that disagreement. A good working relationship is one that can cope with differences. Such a relationship cannot be bought by making substantive concessions or by pretending that disagreements do not exist ... Making an unjustified concession now is unlikely to make it easier to deal with future differences. You may think that next time it [will be] their turn to make a concession; they are likely to believe that if they are stubborn enough, you will again give in.'

- *Negotiate the relationship.* If you don't succeed in establishing such a working relationship, raise your concerns about their behaviour. 'Avoid judging them or impugning their motivations. Rather, explain your perceptions and feelings, and inquire into theirs. Propose external standards or fair principles to determine how you should deal with each other, and decline to give in to pressure tactics. Frame your discussion as looking forward, not back, and operate on the assumptions that [they] may not intend all the consequences you experience, and that they can change their approach if they see the need.'

- *Don't emulate unconstructive behaviour.* 'In most cases, responding in kind reinforces [that] behaviour ... Our behaviour should be designed to model and encourage the behaviour we would prefer, and to avoid any reward for [unconstructive behaviour], both without compromising our substantive interests.'

- *Respond rationally to other people's behaviour even if it seems to be irrational.* Doing so will help you to remain purposeful. And in fact their behaviour may be perfectly rational in the sense of being consistent with their view of the world. If you show some empathy and take their feelings seriously, they may come to a different view.

Cultural traits and differences

In teams made up of people from different cultural backgrounds – different countries, different ethnic groups – it is common for mis-understandings to arise. In growing up with a particular culture, we take on a par-ticular 'mental programming', as Hofstede puts it, giving us a set of 'taken-for-granteds', built-in assumptions about what behaviour is right and proper in various circumstances. As a result, behaviour that is normal to someone brought up in one culture may strike someone brought up in another as being completely out of order, and offence may be taken where none is intended.

In UK universities, a team might comprise students from the 'host community', together with British students who belong to minority ethnic groups, and international students from a variety of countries, for some of whom English is not their mother tongue. There is thus some scope for cultural differences to give rise to misunderstandings.

In this section I focus on certain aspects of culture and cultural differences, and show how misunderstandings can arise. (Of course, they can also arise even in teams drawn from a single culture, often as a result of what we sometimes call 'personality clashes'. I deal with questions of personality in the next section.) I outline these aspects under five headings: (1) Individualism versus collectivism; (2) Tolerance of uncertainty; (3) Issues of embarrassment and 'loss of face'; (4) Issues of gender; and (5) Codes of behaviour. These are shown in Table 8. For the material in this table I have drawn primarily on my own discussions with students and on two very different books: *Cultures and Organizations: Software of the Mind*, by Geert Hofstede,[13] and *Kiss, Bow or Shake Hands: How to Do Business in Sixty Countries*, by Terri Morrison, Wayne A. Conaway and George A. Borden.[14]

Table 8: Cultural traits

Individualism versus collectivism

At one extreme, people brought up in individualist cultures see themselves primarily as individuals. They take it for granted that they have the right to say what they think. They are prepared to confront others with their views, and to take decisions on their own.

At the other extreme, people brought up in collectivist cultures see themselves as members of a family and/or wider group. The preservation of harmony within the group is of major importance. Consequently decisions must command consensus within the group, and taking decisions involves searching for consensus as much as – or rather than – weighing up costs and benefits. Confrontation is avoided.

Tolerance of uncertainty

At one extreme, in some cultures there are authority figures to whom everyone else defers, everyone knows their place, rote learning plays a large part in education. Questioning of authority and critical thinking are discouraged. People brought up in this culture are liable to feel uncomfortable in situations of uncertainty, situations where it is not clear what your place is, what the rules and expectations are, and where there is no 'right answer'.

At the other extreme, there are cultures where authority continually comes under challenge and this is regarded as normal (as is the concomitant bemoaning by older people of the lack of respect shown by the young). Independent and critical thinking are encouraged, up to a point. Instead of having a clearly defined place in society you are playing a game ('snakes and ladders', but with rules that are either invisible or temporary). To some people this, together with the absence of clear rules and expectations and a 'right answer', presents an opportunity and a challenge they can rise to: to others it is baffling and dispiriting.

Issues of embarrassment and 'loss of face'

The feeling of self-consciousness that in English we call 'embarrassment' and the related phenomenon of 'loss of face' seems to be found in all cultures: there is no obvious spectrum running from high embarrassment susceptibility to low. But situations that bring about embarrassment in one culture may have nothing like the same effect in another. You may find it embarrassing to admit that you are unable to perform a particular task; someone from another culture may be able to admit it without the slightest twinge of embarrassment. Similarly you may or may not find it embarrassing to reveal your emotions (especially anger); to express outright disagreement; to refuse to do something when asked; to be unable to understand something that has been said to you more than once; to be discovered not to have told the truth; and/or to attempt to renegotiate an agreement purely in the hope of getting a better deal.

You may also feel embarrassment and loss of face arising out of the way others treat you. Again, people from some cultures may feel these more keenly than those from others. Thus you may or may not find it humiliating if you are not accorded the respect you feel your status deserves; if a contribution that you make to a discussion is not acknowledged; if you suffer a public put-down (e.g. if you ask a question of a speaker and are told 'That's a really silly question!'); and if someone makes a joke at your expense. Cultural differences in sense of humour can constitute a minefield for the unwary: what one person intends as gentle teasing can be experienced by the recipient as a mortal insult.

Issues of gender

It appears that in every culture certain roles and 'places' are assigned to men and to women. Male and female children are treated differently by their parents, undergo some of their (different) socialization in same-sex peer groups, and enter into adulthood with assumptions and expectations as to what behaviour is appropriate for men and for women, and with engrained habits in the way they regard and relate to members of the opposite sex. These assumptions, expectations and habits vary from one culture to another. Consequently, in a team comprising men and women drawn from different cultures, it is very likely that there will be different – indeed, conflicting – assumptions, expectations and habits. For example, some men may find it difficult to 'cope' with women whom they experience as assertive; some women may find it difficult to *be* assertive, or to gauge how assertive it is appropriate for them to be. Women and men from some cultures may simply feel more comfortable and better able to say what they think and feel in the company of others of the same sex.

Codes of behaviour

In all cultures there are codes of behaviour. These label certain kinds of behaviour as acceptable and others as the opposite: unacceptable behaviour may be labelled 'rude', lacking in respect, immodest, and so on, and people feel offended when such behaviour is manifested towards them. Problems arise in teams drawn from more than one culture because what is acceptable in one culture may be unacceptable in another. Some examples are:

- Lack of punctuality

- Boasting

- Standing very close to someone with whom you're conversing

- Gesturing a lot – moving your hands and your head – when talking

- Expressing impatience

- Confrontational behaviour, especially expressing outright disagreement

- Interrupting someone who is talking

- Silences during a conversation. Failure to respond immediately to something that has been said may be interpreted by the speaker as denoting either agreement or disagreement, and may or may not arouse discomfort.

- Failure to maintain eye contact with someone to whom you're talking or listening. When the speaker does this, the listener may erroneously interpret it as denoting insincerity. When the listener does it, the speaker may erroneously interpret it as denoting lack of attentiveness, whereas in fact it is intended to show deference.

As the above examples show, cultural differences have a great capacity for giving rise to misunderstandings. And experience shows that in many multicultural groups such differences do indeed give rise to mis-understandings. If we aren't aware of them, it is all too easy to jump to the conclusion that the other person is being unreasonable, unduly sensitive, or even downright hostile, when in fact they are simply being true to their culture – as you are.

What can be done to minimize such misunderstandings? The first thing, I think, is to appreciate that we are all bearers of our own culture and we are all *prisoners* of our own culture. Our own culture and the assumptions, expectations and taken-for-granteds built into it are blinkers that stop us from comprehending how various kinds of behaviour look and feel from someone else's viewpoint.

But if we have been wearing these blinkers all our lives, we are unaware that we are wearing them. The best way of acquiring that awareness, and going on to shed our blinkers, is by comparing notes with other people from different cultures. In your team, you could compare notes on the cultural traits outlined in Table 8. Which of them apply to which of you? Are there others not mentioned in Table 8 that apply to some of you? How good have you been so far at interpreting each other's signals?

Bear in mind that there is no 'right' or 'superior' culture. None is better than others. It should be possible to make comparisons and discuss them without making any judgments.

Individual traits: 'cats' and 'dogs'

While cultural traits and differences account for many misunderstandings within teams, as you know perfectly well even within a single culture many different types of behaviour can be encountered. Individuals have their own personalities, their own combination of traits, and these lead them to behave in different ways even in very similar situations.

There is a vast literature on the subject of personality and psychoanalysis, but it is not something to get entangled in when you have a group project to deal with. What can be useful, however, is a model that allows us to identify certain kinds of individual traits. Michael Grinder, in his book *Charisma – Cats and Dogs* has produced just such a model.[15] It employs an animal analogy.

Cats and dogs, Grinder reminds us, have very different 'personalities'. 'Cat-oriented people' operate from a position of their own choosing, and hate feeling trapped. They like taking decisions, and are comfortable with power. They like just being themselves. They don't back away from conflict, and if they are the cause of conflict are often unaware of the fact. To get their attention, you need to tease them, to intrigue them. If you try to satisfy them, they get bored.

In contrast, 'dog-oriented people' define themselves in relation to others. They will gather information rather than take decisions, and they shy away from power. They are very aware of others. They may be intimidated and confused by conflict. To get their attention, you need to satisfy them. Tease a dog, and it's liable to turn mean.

Grinder offers these cat and dog 'orientations' as the extreme ends of a continuum. Most people, he argues, can be found at different points on this continuum, depending on the particular contexts: home, work, and so on.

In the particular context of a project group that includes both 'cats' and 'dogs', there is clearly huge scope for them to get on each other's nerves. 'Dogs' may find this conflict particularly upsetting; 'cats' may be impervious to it. The existence of both in the same group is consistent with frequent occurrence of disputes in such groups, and indeed with the prevalence of Tuckman's 'storming'. Arguably, though, to be successful a group needs both, just as Belbin's ideal team requires on the one hand shapers, plants and specialists (cats) and on the other a chairperson, resource investigator, monitor–evaluator, company worker, completer–finisher and team worker (dogs).

This perspective generates some useful advice for both 'cats' and 'dogs'. For 'cats', it must be: remember you're in a team. Please do pay some attention to the feelings of your team-mates. For 'dogs', the advice must be: try not to let the 'cats' wind you up. And don't take their actions as directed at you personally. They're simply indulging in 'cat-behaviour'. Just as we can say of someone 'They are simply being true to their culture', we can also say 'They are simply being true to their personality.'

Part Five

Teamwork issues and solutions

In this part of the book I return to a question-and-answer format, addressing issues that frequently come up with project teams. I've divided them, a little arbitrarily, into two groups: (1) The task: getting the work done; and (2) Personal and interpersonal issues.

The task: getting the work done

In this section I address the following commonly arising issues:

- Getting help from your teachers
- Sharing the work load: 'social loafing'
- The 'free rider' problem
- Focusing on the task
- Taking decisions: 'risky shift', 'group polarization' and 'groupthink'

Getting help from your teachers

I know it's supposed to be 'our' project, but does that mean we can't ask our teachers for help?

Different teachers are likely to have different views on this, but you will always get further if you first clarify what it is that you want.

An all-purpose, non-specific cry of 'Help!' will probably get you nowhere. But if, for example, you are faced with a problem that you have to solve, and you ask for help with elucidating and understanding the problem – clearing up an ambiguity, say – you are more likely to get a helpful response than if you ask for help with solving it.

Similarly, if your teachers do offer assistance while you're working on the project, and you can't make up your minds which of two avenues to pursue, don't ask your teachers: 'Which one is better?' Think about *how* to choose between them, then ask your teachers: 'Are these the right criteria to use in making our choice?' Teachers tend to respond more favourably to students who show some initiative than to those who just want to be told what to do. Cultivating helplessness is not a productive strategy in this situation.

And bear in mind that teachers have to be sure they are providing a 'level playing field': they can't give – or let it appear that they are giving – favoured treatment to any one team.

It may conceivably happen that you ask more than one person for help and get different answers. This can happen because what people are giving you is simply their opinion, and it allows you to choose which opinion you prefer. But if, say, you get different interpretations of something in your project brief, the situation is more serious, and you must do your best to resolve the discrepancy. Take your difficulty to the most senior person you can find, explain the difficulty, and ask for an authoritative statement. In my view, you are unquestionably entitled to do this.

Sharing the work load: 'social loafing'

Two of us seem to be doing all the work. What's gone wrong?

Two members of our so-called team have taken charge of our project. I feel that I'm not valued and consequently I don't feel motivated to exert myself.

It is almost inevitable that at some times in the progress of a project some people will be doing more work than others. To take a simple example, the member who has been allocated the task of editing the final report may be doing relatively little early on while everybody else is getting stuck in, and then shouldering the whole burden in the last few days (and nights).

But it may be that some 'social loafing' is going on. Psychologists have found that – in some cultures, at least – people working in a group put less effort into tackling a task than if they are tackling it on their own.[16] Especially where the task is simple, everyone is doing the same thing, individual contributions are not identifiable, or people may get in each other's way, there seems to be an innate tendency for us not to work as hard as we otherwise would. So check that none of these conditions is present in your case.

It does sometimes happen that a couple of people – with more advanced technical skills, perhaps, or a shared idea for the product – effectively take charge of the project, and the others begin to feel they're being shut out. The 'taking over' may not come about deliberately; if you are one of the 'activists' you are perhaps being carried along by your own enthusiasm and putting in two or three times as many hours as the other members. And you may be completely unaware – especially if you're a 'cat' and/or 'shaper' – how the others are feeling.

If you are not one of the activists, you are very likely to feel unvalued, or undervalued. It is not surprising in such circumstances that your motivation drops, and you don't work as hard or enthusiastically as you are capable of doing. Indeed, you may be unable to see how you can make a contribution in these circumstances.

This situation has to be talked about. You have to put it on the agenda for a meeting of the whole team. Each of you has to say how you see the situation and how you feel about it. Note that is not – I repeat, *not* – a subject for accusation or blaming. Indeed, statements beginning 'You are. . .' should be avoided. What you can and should say is: 'This is how I see the situation, and this is how I feel about it . . .' The only person who is an authority on your perceptions and feelings is yourself, and you must speak up for yourself: no one can speak for you. And by the same token, you can speak for no one else.

Once perceptions and feelings are out in the open, and the air is cleared, you can compare your perceptions of what's going on. Are some individual tasks turning out to involve much more work than originally envisaged? Are the activists indeed charging along fuelled by their own enthusiasm? Is it indeed unclear what role the others can be taking on now?

Then it's time to turn to the question: how shall we proceed from this point on? Do you need to do more to acknowledge members' contributions? Do you need to make a fresh assessment of what tasks need to be carried out, and/or revise the allocation of tasks to individuals or pairs? Can some team members join in with the 'fun' work? Could some take on more of the workload later? Maybe those who have been feeling excluded will recover their motivation and involvement if the two activists carry on as they have been but make a point of reporting regularly to the others and consulting them on any issues they are faced with.

You might also like to review your mission statement and the basis on which jobs were initially allocated. No doubt you still want to do the best project you can, but is everybody learning as much as they can or wish? Did some people take on more than, with hindsight, they should have done, and did others take on less?

The 'free-rider' problem

One member of our team is not pulling his weight. He doesn't say much in meetings, and when he says he will do something doesn't produce the goods. He seems to be taking advantage of the fact that we will all get the same mark for our project, so however little he does he will benefit from the work the rest of us do. It's both unfair and highly irritating.

'Free-riding' is the name given to the behaviour of a team member who deliberately limits the work that he or she puts in, in the knowledge that they will nevertheless benefit from the efforts of the other members. (It's the conscious equivalent of 'social loafing'.) If your teachers have given some thought to the possibility that some students might try to take a free ride, they may have tried to maximize the incentive to work as a team by providing for a proportion of marks to come from a self- and peer-assessment. Students can be asked to evaluate the contributions of themselves and other team members in terms of attendance at meetings, interaction with others (including facilitating contributions by others), planning the project, leadership and management, and contributing to producing the deliverables. The idea is to make each of you more aware of how you are regarded by other members of your group. A marking system can be adopted which disregards a self-assessment that is appreciably higher (or lower) on any criterion than the aggregate assessment of that student supplied by the other members of the group.

In the absence of such a marking scheme, or if there is such a scheme but it isn't having the intended effect, what can you do?

The first thing, I suggest, is to find out what's in the supposedly free-riding student's mind. Perhaps just one of you could talk to him (rather than summoning him to a 'trial by his peers'). It may turn out that he feels under pressure to devote more time and effort to the project than he feels is appropriate, and is backing out of doing the work entailed. So he may appear to be free-riding although he has no intention of taking advantage of the work of the rest of you. If this is the case you need to have a full and frank discussion, in the whole team, to find a way forward.

It may also be that when tasks were allocated the noisier and more forceful members of the group were the first to bid for those that they preferred, and that the quietest, most diffident member found himself left with a task for which he felt very ill-equipped, but he nevertheless felt it his duty to take it on and did so, while keeping his fingers crossed that he would be able to master it. If he subsequently floundered, he may have been reluctant to ask for help, and instead withdrew: not turning up to meetings, not replying to emails, etc. Almost certainly he is experiencing a great deal of discomfort and stress, but the rest of you may conclude that he is deliberately free-riding. A quiet talk may uncover what is really going on, and then you can have a constructive discussion of how best to remedy the situation and welcome him back into the team.

If you have evidence that there is some free-riding going on, a deliberate taking advantage of the rest of you and your hard work, it is – in my view – perfectly appropriate to let your teachers know about the situation and ask for their help in dealing with it.

Perhaps, however, you feel that the issue is one that you should deal with yourselves. The important thing to deal with is not the behaviour of the free-rider but your own feelings. It would not be surprising if you feel very angry, and frustrated by the uncertainty which is inevitable when someone takes away his individual tasks and then goes quiet and fails to come back to the group with the work he has done, or keeps making excuses but promises to deliver 'soon'. In this situation you don't know whether to do the work yourselves or to trust the other member and hold the project in abeyance until he or she produces, and to hope that what is produced will be what you need. The problem may be not so much that one member is unreliable and unproductive – aggravating though that is – but that the conscientious members are crippled by their feelings of anger towards the free-rider and of frustration resulting from their inability to influence events and from their dependence on the free-rider.

In such a situation, your first priority has to be to free yourself from your dependence on the free-rider. Your strategy might include: asking the free-rider if he is encountering difficulties that he hasn't made known to the other members of the team; explaining to the free-rider your difficulty with the situation you find yourselves in; giving the free-rider a deadline for the producing of work; and agreeing among yourselves how you will do the work if it is not forthcoming from him.

Above all, though, you need a contingency plan. Not a contingency plan for what you will do if the free-rider doesn't produce, but a contingency plan for what you will do if he *does*. Plan your work programme on the basis that he *won't* produce (make sure, though, that you tell him what you are doing and why), but be prepared to react flexibly if – to your amazement – he does come up with the goods.

Dealing with free-riders can actually be a worthwhile learning experience for you, if you can develop strategies to channel your anger and frustration into positive action.

Focusing on the task

I'm keen to make a success of our project, but everyone else seems more concerned to achieve agreement and maintain a friendly atmosphere. It's very discouraging. What can I do?

Sometimes groups do seem more concerned to achieve agreement and maintain a friendly atmosphere than to come up with a really good product. Whether intentionally or not, the needs of the team are taking priority over the demands of the task. It may be that there's a kind of displacement activity taking place: are people shying away from facing up to the task – with its difficulty and its potential for causing disagreement – and putting their energy into social activity instead? If you think this is the case, why not write a note on the task, perhaps setting out what you see the brief as calling for and suggesting how the overall task could be broken down into smaller ones, and circulate this note with a polite covering letter saying you'd be really interested in other people's ideas? It could be that taking the initiative in this way is all that's needed to get people started.

Is it possible, though, that you're being somewhat impatient? Maybe the others are sensibly paying attention to creating a 'social infrastructure' for the team, and that this will pay dividends in terms of helping the team to keep together when you all get down to serious work. If this is the process that's taking place, be sure that you are playing your part in it. If you are established as a fully paid-up member of the team, any note that you write and circulate will get a more welcoming response. You're likely to find that everyone would like the team to be purposeful as well as good-humoured.

Taking decisions: 'risky shift', 'group polarization' and 'groupthink'

Several times we've taken decisions which have subsequently proved to be unwise, so we waste time and effort and have to backtrack. What can we do to get decisions right first time?

We've got a very persuasive talker in our team, and I think sometimes we get swept along into taking decisions without considering them properly. How can we avoid this?

Psychologists have found that groups of people taking collective decisions tend to make more extreme choices – either more risky (the so-called 'risky shift') or more cautious – than their members would make if taking the decision on their own.[17] This phenomenon has been labelled 'group polarization'. It can happen without anyone exerting pressure.

What successful pressurizers do is to create a situation where for you to oppose their proposal would be to disrupt the team and make life difficult for yourself. So to do so would be contrary to the needs of the team and your own individual needs. Where everyone who isn't pressurizing succumbs to the pressure, the resultant team behaviour is known as 'groupthink'.[18]

So what can you do? Here are some suggestions:

- Notice that decisions get taken in response to 'issues', perceptions of situations where there is an imperative: 'We've got to take a decision. Something must be done!' However forcefully the issue is being pressed upon you, always be prepared to challenge an issue that you are presented with. *Does* something need to be done? Why? Do you need to decide *right now* what to do?

- Never let yourself be 'bounced' into taking a decision before you feel you've considered it properly. You might like to make it a ground rule that anyone who comes to a team meeting seeking a decision *must* circulate at least 24 hours beforehand a note setting out all the relevant considerations, so the rest of you have a chance to think about them. It's very probable that someone who is trying to bounce you into a decision has their own personal reasons for doing so. They aren't necessarily reasons that would appeal to you too.

- Never take a decision without considering alternatives. Always ask: 'What could we do instead?' There will rarely be no alternative at all.

- Always evaluate alternatives coolly and systematically. Ask: 'What are the likely consequences of each alternative? What are the right criteria to use in choosing between them?'

- Resist the pressurizers. Work out your preferences individually, then get together and pool your thoughts to reach your collective decision.

Personal and interpersonal issues

In this section I address the following commonly arising issues:

- The group that doesn't storm
- Getting your multicultural group to 'bond'
- Do teams need leaders?
- Dealing with a team member who tries to dominate
- Working constructively with someone you don't like
- Finding your place in the team

The group that doesn't storm

Our group seems to have moved without trouble from forming to norming and now performing. So we haven't been storming: is there something wrong with us?

Not going through a storming phase might indicate that you're a bunch of sensitive, mature people, who are aware of your own abilities and needs, able to put yourselves in other people's shoes and calmly negotiate differences. Or that you're evenly matched in terms of the skills and commitment that you're bringing to your project, and that your skills are complementary, with minimal overlap. So you've met little stress, and are well able to deal with what stress has arisen.

But it could also mean that there is hidden conflict: it hasn't surfaced yet. Perhaps you're still in the forming stage. Ask yourselves these questions: is anyone bottling up strong feelings, which are likely to burst out at some point? Have you divided up the overall task in a way that gives everyone their own individual task but does not respect the complexity of the overall task, so there are bound to be clashes ahead? Does your team lack a 'plant' or 'shaper' who creates dissension but also contributes creativity? If you answer 'yes' to any of these questions, then the sooner you take action – encourage everyone to say how they're feeling, review your division of labour, and brainstorm for creative ideas – the better.

Getting your multicultural group to 'bond'

We're a mixed group of women and men from five different countries. Some of us are quite outgoing, others rather shy and reserved. What can we do to help us 'bond' and generate some team spirit?

You need, as I think you realize, to pay some attention to your social infrastructure. Make a point of doing some things as a group. Have coffee, have a meal together, regularly. Go to a movie. Organize a picnic or other outing. (Decide collectively what you're going to do.) Learning to relax in each other's company will help you to bond.

At the same time, you're well aware that your group consists of five individuals. Within the group, there are accordingly ten one-to-one relationships. Books on teamwork tend to ignore these relationships, but if only one of them is a hostile relationship it can poison the whole team. So each of you should make a point of getting to know the other four on an individual basis. Take opportunities to talk, show an interest in them, check out your respective cultural traits and differences. Even if you find someone 'difficult', it's worth persevering and doing what you can to gain their confidence.

Finally, don't concentrate on social matters to the exclusion of the task. Your task will inevitably be a source of some anxiety, especially at the beginning. So get together early on to compare your thoughts on how to tackle your project and plan your initial work. Doing some actual work together is a good way of developing team spirit.

Do teams need leaders?

A couple of people in our team feel strongly that we ought to choose a leader. I'm instinctively against it. I can't see how to resolve our disagreement.

The question to ask the supporters of choosing a leader is this: What do we need a leader *for*? Or, to be more specific, if we had a leader, what would we want that person to *do*?

If you get straightforward answers to these questions, they are likely to show that the supporters feel there is a problem (or more than one) in the team. Maybe they feel you are all pulling in different directions, or that meetings are ending without decisions being taken. If this is the case, ask yourselves if there are other ways of solving the problem without choosing a leader. Perhaps the problem could be solved by giving the most suitable person responsibility for chairing meetings – but stopping short of appointing that person 'leader' – and having regular 'coordination meetings' to ensure you're all working on the same 'big picture' and in tune with one another. Maybe you could all take responsibility for carrying out the functions that a 'leader' might perform. And when it comes to particular issues or tasks, you may find that different people take on the leadership role according to their expertise or grasp of the situation. It may be best to allow these leadership roles to emerge and move around within the team, rather than to designate someone to take on the leadership in every situation.

If you *don't* get straightforward answers to these questions, it could mean that those who support choosing a leader don't want responsibility – they would rather put it all on the leader – or that someone objects to the way things have been going and is making a bid for power. It's better to bring out and discuss the underlying problems than to assume that choosing a leader will solve them. Once you have a leader, deposing him or her could be a messy business that will destroy the team and distract you from your task.

Dealing with a team member who tries to dominate

We have someone in our team whose behaviour in meetings is quite objectionable. He talks a lot, loud and fast, and behaves very impatiently and aggressively towards anyone who questions him or disagrees with him. A couple of members of our team are quite intimidated by him. How can we bring him under control?

If you've never before had to work with someone like this, finding you've been put in a group with them can be very disconcerting. As you say, you may find their behaviour in meetings quite objectionable, and be puzzled as to how best to deal with them.

First of all, see what you can find to appreciate about this character. He evidently has energy: does he have a clear vision of the project and how to go about it; does he bring valuable technical skills to it; when he promises to do a piece of work by the next meeting does he actually get it done and produce it? If the answer to these questions is 'no', you are dealing with a blusterer and a bully, and the longer you tolerate him the more distracting and tiring you will find him. So you have to face up to him: the sooner, the better.

One thing you can do is the 'Are we a team?' exercise (see page 55), which will provide an opportunity for everyone to express their feelings and for the would-be dominator to realize how he is perceived by the other members. Something else that the rest of you can do is to get together and produce a draft work programme for all of you, then table this at a team meeting. He now has the option of suggesting alterations or not, and joining in or not. And the rest of you can see what he does and proceed accordingly.

Incidentally, don't have any qualms about meeting 'behind his back'. It is more important to look after the two people who are being intimidated, and you can say precisely that if challenged.

If you're clear that the character you're dealing with does have something of value to contribute to the team – energy, vision, skills and so on – the challenge for the rest of you is to keep him in, 'civilize' him a bit if possible, and master the feelings of discomfort that he has been inducing in you up to now. Evidently he is a 'cat' person, so learn to think of him as a valuable pet. He behaves as he does because that's the way he is: his behaviour may be culturally quite alien to you, especially if you've been brought up in a culture where harmony is valued, but if you can regard him as the bit of grit in the oyster that may produce a pearl you'll find that you are able to surmount your original reaction. And if you can control the decision-making process – insist on papers being prepared, always consider alternatives and compare them carefully – you should be able to avoid being stampeded into decisions if he gets into 'dominating' mode.

Working constructively with someone you don't like

I'm in a team with someone I just don't like. I don't think she likes me. It's an uncomfortable situation. Is there anything I can do to make it less uncomfortable?

In the world of work you may well find yourself assigned to a team that includes one or more people whom you do not particularly like. They may not particularly like you! And if there's a tension between the two of you it may be making life uncomfortable for everyone else in the team too. Nevertheless you all have to work together. And working together will very probably be vital to the success of your current project. Here are some suggestions for managing the situation.

- Focus your attention on the job in hand: the overall task and the individual tasks which fall to you. There is work to be done!

- Stick to the ground rules which your team has adopted (if it hasn't adopted any, suggest that it does so) and work on the assumption that other members will do so too. If there are agreed ways of doing things, you are less likely to be annoyed by what other people do.

● In your mind, try to divorce the person from her behaviour. You can feel critical of what someone does without letting that person become a 'bogeyman' to you.

● Try to find something that you can value and appreciate in the person you don't like. It is unlikely that there is absolutely *nothing* that she can usefully contribute.

● See if it is possible to decrease your sensitivity to the person you don't like. Her attitudes and behaviour will reflect her culture and personality, just as your reaction will reflect yours. Use your brain to try to explain to yourself what is going on; try to understand it. Once you have transformed your reaction from 'She is so objectionable' to 'How interesting that what she does has such an effect on me', you will have decreased your sensitivity to a fraction of what it was.

Finding your place in the team

In my team I'm the oldest and have most experience of teamwork, so it clearly makes sense for me to be the leader. Why don't the other members agree with me?

I find it difficult to contribute to discussion and other collective activities. A couple of times I've made a suggestion and nobody paid any attention, then five minutes later someone else made the same suggestion and people said: 'What a good idea.' I feel not just snubbed but invisible. What should I do?

In a newly created team, with no designated leader, everyone ostensibly starts off on an equal footing, but we bring all sorts of assumptions about status, rights and obligations – ours and other people's – and I suspect we do quite a lot of comparing and ranking when forming first impressions of one another. In the climate of a new project, there is a great deal of uncertainty, and it's natural to seek the reassurance that goes with a position in a hierarchy. And then to feel resentment when someone else seems to be taking a position that you feel is rightfully yours. Some people distance themselves from the group when that happens. Other people – more modest or diffident, perhaps – become self-effacing, and look to other people for clues as to where they fit in.

Arguably, a student project team – if it is to be effective – has to be 'organic' (see page 74). Its structure will be shaped at any given time by the issues that are being faced and the tasks that are being undertaken. You should be able to gain the reassurance you need from feeling that you are fully participating in the decision-making and substantive work of your team, as well as from any little acknowledgments that come your way.

It has to be said that many students are not very good at acknowledging the contributions of others. Being educated in institutions where a culture of individual achievement largely prevails, and being taught by academics who are more accustomed to deliver criticism than appreciation, are not conducive to learning to register, appreciate and acknowledge the contributions that other people make. Assertive males from individualist cultures are particularly likely to be deficient in this respect, sometimes to the point where they don't even notice contributions made by modest females from collectivist cultures.

So what can you do to make your mark and get noticed? Here are some suggestions:

- When you have done a piece of work, make sure you present it clearly and strikingly, and circulate copies, so that everyone is aware of what you have done. Good presentation is crucial to ensure it isn't overlooked.

- Before a meeting when an issue is coming up, clarify for yourself what you think are the relevant considerations, get them on to paper (or screen), and circulate them. Take some paper copies to meetings for people who haven't checked their email. If you're not confident in English, use notes or bullet points, where grammar is not important.

- In meetings, if you are seeking a particular decision be sure to state clearly what it is that you want. Sit forward on your chair; don't lean back. If someone else is talking and you want clarification, raise your hand and keep it up. If you are ignored, say: 'Excuse me!' If you are still ignored, keep saying it, over and over, until everyone else is quiet. Cultivate short and pithy questions and comments: 'How can you tell?' 'What is your evidence for that?' 'Have you considered doing it another way?' 'I'd like to offer an alternative.'

- Do your bit to encourage and facilitate contributions from other team members. This will help to set the 'tone' for the team, and you will find them doing the same for you.
- Bear in mind and make allowances for the cultural and individual traits of others, especially for what may strike you as their poor social skills.

Part Six

Benefiting from the experience

This part of the book deals with some carry-overs and follow-ups. It contains three sections: (1) Getting feedback – including appreciation; (2) Reflective reports and learning logs; and (3) Applying for jobs.

Getting feedback – including appreciation

It's impossible to predict how the members of a team will feel when their project comes to an end. If you finish in a rush right up to the deadline, your feelings are likely to be a mixture of relief, exhilaration and exhaustion, in proportions varying according to how big a part you've been playing in the final stages. And you may feel very close to your team-mates; or you may feel you never want to set eyes on them again.

If you're carrying any negative feelings with you – perhaps something that someone said or did during the project is still 'bugging' you – it would be really good to 'exorcise' them, to get them out of your system. Here's something you can do.

Arrange a post-project meeting of your team, at a time convenient to everyone and in a calm, quiet place. At the meeting, sit in a circle. Take it in turns to say how you're feeling about the project, and in particular if anything is bugging you, an aggravation that you can't get out of your mind. The rule is that you can say how you see things (your perceptions) and how you're feeling, and you can say what your reaction was to a team-mate's behaviour, but you're not allowed to make accusations, to use words like 'blame' and 'fault', or to express judgments about another person's behaviour.

If, say, you and someone else have fallen out, and the disagreement hasn't yet been resolved, it's an opportunity for the two of you to state your impressions of what happened and say how it left you feeling, with the others 'holding the ring' and seeing the rules are kept to. Otherwise they should keep quiet, at least until the two of you have had your say. You should then go on to consider ways in which you could have done things differently (the others can join in at this point).

Almost certainly you'll find that this process has a cathartic effect. Even if you end up having to agree to differ, you are most unlikely to feel as bugged afterwards as you did before.

Finally, here's a nice way to end: the 'circle of appreciation'. Still sitting in your circle, go round the circle with each team member in turn telling each of the others one or two things that he or she has appreciated about the contribution he or she has made to the work of the team. This is a moment for positives: it would be extraordinary if you were unable to find at least one positive thing to say about everyone.

(When you read this in cold print, does it sound a bit touchy-feely, or even unBritish? By the time you have gone through a project together, through the highs and lows, it won't be a difficult thing to do. And given how strongly criticism is emphasized in UK universities, some words of appreciation will make a heart-warming change, as well as allowing you to end your project on a high note.)

Reflection

Learning logs

Some students doing group projects are required to keep a 'learning log' – a daily journal – during their project, documenting their activities, learning, etc. Some find themselves with detailed instructions about this: so detailed, indeed, that complying with them could become both onerous and a distraction from the project. I commend the idea of keeping a diary, but suggest that you keep it very simple. Use the 'How am I doing?' questionnaire in Box 6 as a checklist of things to cover.

Reflective reports

An alternative or supplement to the learning log is the 'reflective report', written after the project has been completed. Many students who have written reflective reports have found that in writing it they were reflecting deeply on how their team worked and their part in it, and it is clear from the many reports I have read that valuable insights can be gained from this exercise. If you would like to have a go at one, for your own benefit, here are some guidelines for you.

As a rough guide, aim to write between 1250 and 1750 words (i.e. 1500 +/− 250 words). This is big enough for you to get into the subject, but shouldn't be so big as to be intimidating. The report should set out what you personally have learned about teamwork from your experience on this project. It should include:

- a brief description of the members of your team, a chronology of the main events, and the main issues that arose and how they were tackled;
- your best shot at explaining why what happened did happen;
- an outline of the lessons you have learned and what you would do differently given another opportunity to tackle the project.

If you want to go further into the subject, you could set all this in the context of research findings and debate in the literature on teams and organizations, using the material in Part Four of this book and consulting some of the further reading listed on pages 125–7. You could also compare and contrast this team experience with any previous team experience that you have had.

If you aren't actually required to write a reflective report, what you write will be for no one else's eyes but yours and you can be as frank as you wish. If you *are* required to write one, which your teachers will read, I suggest you anonymize it by referring to your team-mates as A, B, C . . .

Applying for jobs

When you've had some teamwork experience, you doubtless want to make the most of it when applying for jobs. There are three elements of this process that I want to cover: (1) Polishing up your CV (or resume in North America); (2) Being interviewed; and (3) Taking part in group exercises in assessment centres.

Polishing up your CV

When you have had some experience of group projects, it's a very good idea to say something about it in your *curriculum vitae*, your resume. It is, after all, a qualification that you possess. The very fact that you have participated in a group project will probably catch the recruiter's eye, and may help to get you on to a shortlist. So include in your CV a note of the fact that you have taken part in one or more group projects as part of your academic work. If the subject matter is relevant to the job you're applying for, outline it briefly. If you played a particular role, you could mention that too.

If you're applying for a job where you have to complete an application form and they don't want a CV from you, find the most suitable place to insert this information. This could be in a section headed 'academic qualifications', or one headed 'other relevant information'.

Being interviewed

If you've mentioned your teamwork experience on your CV or application form, and you're called for interview, it's highly likely that you'll be asked about it. So you've got to be prepared for questions.

What might you be asked? One obvious question is: what lessons did you learn from doing your group project? You might also be asked: did you enjoy the project? What aspects in particular did you enjoy? What role did you play in the team? Do you feel you're well equipped for any particular team role? What issues did you face and how did you overcome them?

So before the interview think about how you would answer these and similar questions. If you have written a reflective report for yourself, dig it out and reread it to remind yourself about the experience.

Go easy when telling interviewers what you have learned. Don't make a claim like 'I have learned how to be a good team player', which could be interpreted as meaning you think you have nothing more to learn on the subject. You want to invite the response 'Tell us more', not 'Who do you think you are?' Something like 'I think I've gained some sense of what it means to be a good team player' would be more appropriate (in the UK, at least).

On the off-chance that the interviewers don't ask you about teamwork, take an opportunity to raise it yourself. For example, if they say to you 'Is there anything you'd like to ask us?', you can ask them whether your teamwork experience would be relevant to the job.

Group exercises in assessment centres

If you are a final-year student looking for a job with a major employer, and you've got through the initial screening and on to a shortlist, there's a good chance that you'll be invited along to an assessment centre for a day, and that part of the day will be taken up with a group exercise. How should you prepare for this?

First, notice what employers *say* they are looking for: good team players, good communicators, people who can 'hit the ground running', and so on.

Second, be aware what they are usually *actually* looking for: people who will 'fit in' to their organization, feel 'at home' with the people already working for them, and generally be happy cooperating with others.

This last is the clue. The culture of the workplace – or at least the culture that many employers would like to have in their workplace, which is what shows up at assessment centres – is a culture of *cooperation*. And this culture is literally a world away from the 'individual achievement' culture of higher education. There are other differences too. Out in the real world the focus is on tangible products, not examination answers. People are concerned with issues, not abstractions. Interaction 'up and down' takes place in meetings, not lecture theatres.

The effect of all this is that when you go into the group exercise room you are in for a culture shock. If you haven't worked in a group before, you are in for a *massive* culture shock. And of course there's no way that anyone who's in the throes of a culture shock can perform at their best, especially if they don't even know what the assessors are looking for.

What can you do to prepare? If you've been involved in group projects as part of your academic work, you have a head start, but you *must* be able to stand back from the experience. So look back and ask yourself: what went well? What didn't go so well? What would I do differently, given the chance again?

Don't shy away from assessment centres. Get to as many as you can manage and spare time for, even with employers you don't think you want to end up working for. It's another way of getting group experience. You will certainly perform better at your fifth one than at your first.

Finally, remember the different team-building and team-maintenance roles that people perform in groups:

- *Organizer*: Keeps meetings focused and in order, determined to get through the agenda.

- *Encourager*: Brings good-humoured appreciation to proceedings, able to defuse tensions and revive flagging morale.

- *Facilitator*: Ensures that the quieter members of the group are heard and everyone's contribution is acknowledged.

- *Recorder*: Keeps a note of decisions (especially decisions as to who will do what before the next meeting); ensures that everyone is aware of them.

- *Time-keeper and progress-chaser*: Keeps an eye on the clock.

- *Coordinator*: Sees the 'big picture' (the strategic overview), has an eye for gaps and overlaps.

- *Lookout*: Visualizes future scenarios, is alert to issues that may be looming over the horizon.

It's performance in these roles, as well as the contribution of ideas and suggestions, that assessors at group exercises watch out for. Watch out for them yourself, and develop the knack of taking up any role that's going begging. The assessors will be impressed, and you'll enjoy yourself. What better outcome could there be?

Box 7

Web links, feedback, updates

Links to useful websites can be found by logging on to

www.student-friendly-guides.com

If you have any questions about projects and teamwork that this book hasn't covered, or any suggestions for improving it, please log on to the website and email them to me. I'll be glad to answer any questions, and all suggestions for improvements will be very gratefully received.

And don't forget to check out the website regularly for updates to this and other student-friendly guides.

Notes and references

1   R. Meredith Belbin, *Management Teams: Why They Succeed or Fail* (Oxford 1981, subsequently republished by Butterworth-Heinemann), p. 10 in the republished version.

2   John Adair, *Effective Teambuilding: How to Make a Winning Team* (Pan 1987), p. 60.

3   Belbin, *Management Teams: Why They Succeed or Fail* (see note 1) and *Team Roles at Work* (Butterworth-Heinemann 1993).

4   Belbin, *Management Teams: Why They Succeed or Fail* (see note 1), p. 150.

5   Belbin, *Management Teams: Why They Succeed or Fail* (see note 1), p. 74.

6   Kenneth D. Benne and Paul Sheats, 'Functional roles of group members', *Journal of Social Issues* (1948), Vol. 4, No. 2, pp. 41–9.

7   Tom Burns and G.M. Stalker, *The Management of Innovation* (2nd edition, Tavistock 1966), p. vii.

8   Burns and Stalker (see note 7), pp. 119–22.

9   Bruce W. Tuckman, 'Developmental sequence in small groups', *Psychological Bulletin* (1965), Vol. 63, No. 6, pp. 384–99. This says 50 articles were reviewed. The later publication (see note 10) says 55 articles were reviewed in the original study.

10   Bruce W. Tuckman and Mary Ann C. Jensen, 'Stages of small-group development revisited', *Group and Organization Studies* (1977), Vol. 2, No. 4, pp. 419–27.

11   For more on the subject of 'commitment', see P.H. Levin, *Government and the Planning Process* (George Allen and Unwin 1976), Chs 2 and 3, and Peter Levin, *Making Social Policy* (Open University Press 1997), Ch. 4.

12   Roger Fisher and William Ury (and, for the second edition, Bruce Patton), *Getting to Yes: Negotiating an Agreement Without Giving In* (Arrow 1997).

13   Geert Hofstede, *Cultures and Organizations: Software of the Mind* (McGraw-Hill 1997).

14   Terri Morrison, Wayne A. Conaway and George A. Borden, *Kiss, Bow or Shake Hands: How to Do Business in Sixty Countries* (Adams Media 1994).

15   Michael Grinder, *Charisma – Cats and Dogs* (Michael Grinder and Associates 2003).

16   For a concise run-down on social loafing, see Andrzej Huczynski and David Buchanan, *Organizational Behaviour: An Introductory Text* (4th edition, Prentice Hall 2001), pp. 352–3.

17   Huczynski and Buchanan, *Organizational Behaviour: An Introductory Text* (see note 16), pp. 752–5.

18   Huczynski and Buchanan, *Organizational Behaviour: An Introductory Text* (see note 16), pp. 755–8. The classic work on groupthink is Irving L. Janis, *Groupthink: Psychological Studies of Policy Decisions and Fiascoes* (2nd edition, Houghton Mifflin 1982).

Further reading

A select list of useful books and articles is given below. It is divided into five parts:

- 'How to' books for team leaders and members
- Textbooks on project management (for Gantt charts, critical path analysis, etc.)
- Research and other studies of teamwork
- Organizational behaviour and social psychology texts with chapters on, or relevant to, teamwork
- Books on cultural traits and cultural differences

'How to' books for team leaders and members

John Adair, *Effective Teambuilding: How to Make a Winning Team* (Pan 1987). The first half of the book is on understanding groups and individuals, the second on building and maintaining high-performance teams. Lots of practical advice for actual and potential team leaders.

Roland and Frances Bee, *Project Management: The People Challenge* (Institute of Personnel and Development 1997). Particularly good on project teams and setting teamwork issues in the context of a complex project where the overall task has to be broken down into many sub-tasks. See also the same authors' *Constructive Feedback* (Institute of Personnel and Development 1996).

Michael West, *Effective Teamwork* (British Psychological Society 1994). A concise and practical book for people who find themselves in teams. Contains some useful techniques and exercises.

Roger Fisher and William Ury, with Bruce Patton, *Getting to Yes: Negotiating an Agreement Without Giving In* (2nd edition, Arrow 1997). Will help you to do what the title says.

Textbooks on project management (for Gantt charts, critical path analysis, etc.)

Sang M. Lee and Marc J. Schniederjans, *Operations Management* (Houghton Mifflin 1994)

Steven Nahmias, *Production and Operations Analysis* (McGraw-Hill 2001)
Nigel Slack, Stuart Chambers and Robert Johnston, *Operations Management* (FT Prentice Hall 2003)

Research and other studies of teamwork

R. Meredith Belbin, *Management Teams: Why They Succeed or Fail* (Oxford 1981, re-issued by Butterworth-Heinemann 1996). Seminal work on team roles.

R. Meredith Belbin, *Team Roles at Work* (Butterworth-Heinemann 1993). Follow-up to his earlier book.

Michael Colenso (ed.), *Kaizen Strategies for Improving Team Performance* (Financial Times/Prentice-Hall 2000). *Kaizen* started as a Japanese management system which grew out of the quality movement, but in its present form amounts to an organizational culture which is very congruent with team-working. An invaluable book for a student with experience of teamwork who wants to develop his or her business awareness.

Charles Handy, *Understanding Organizations* (4th edition, Penguin 1993). Of particular interest are Chapter 3 ('On roles and interactions') and Chapter 6 ('On the workings of groups').

P. Kettley and W. Hirsh, *Learning from Cross-Functional Teamwork* (Institute for Employment Studies, Report 356, 2000). Report on a study of how members of cross-functional teams learn, examining the impact on the learning process and learning outcomes of organizational culture and systems and of the operating principles and dynamic of the team.

Stephen Procter and Frank Mueller (eds), *Teamwork* (Macmillan 2000). A collection of papers on research into teamwork in industry. Those on the experiences and attitudes of employees who have had teamwork 'done' to them are a valuable complement to the 'how to' materials written for managers.

Organizational behaviour and social psychology texts with chapters on, or relevant to, teamwork

Andrzej Huczynski and David Buchanan, *Organizational Behaviour: An Introductory Text* (4th edition, Prentice-Hall 2001)

Robert Kreitner, Angelo Kinicki and Marc Buelens, *Organizational Behaviour: Second European Edition* (McGraw-Hill 2002)

Eliot R. Smith and Diane M. Mackie, *Social Psychology* (2nd edition, Psychology Press 2000)

Joseph W. Weiss, *Organizational Behavior and Change: Managing Diversity, Cross-cultural Dynamics, and Ethics* (2nd edition, South-Western College Publishing 2001)

Books on cultural traits and cultural differences

Geert Hofstede, *Cultures and Organizations: Software of the Mind* (McGraw-Hill 1991)

Robert Kreitner, Angelo Kinicki and Marc Buelens, *Organizational Behaviour: Second European Edition* (McGraw Hill 2002), Chs 4 and 5

Colin Lago and Alison Barty, *Working with International Students: A Cross-cultural Training Manual* (UKCOSA: The Council for International Education 2003)

Terri Morrison, Wayne A. Conaway and George A. Borden, *Kiss, Bow or Shake Hands: How to Do Business in Sixty Countries* (Adams Media 1994). Unfortunately the 60 countries don't include any African ones.

Background and acknowledgments

This book has grown out of my personal involvement in teamwork initiatives in higher education dating back to 1995, when I first took part as a tutor in the Team Development in Universities programme funded by BP and carried out in 12 UK universities by Mike Rawlins and Peter Danby, 'Chalybeate'. This made use of two-day outdoor courses and drew heavily for its inspiration on the Kolb 'experiential learning cycle'. The great majority of students found the course both challenging and highly enjoyable, and showed me that outdoor team training courses could be very productive in terms of enhancing students' personal development and giving them an experience of 'team bonding' under stress. But there was some evidence that on returning to the academic environment students 'revert to type': if they are given no encouragement to bring teamwork skills to their academic work it is not easy for them to see how to do this of their own accord, and they go back to working as individuals. Moreover I became increasingly doubtful whether teamwork in experiential learning could be transferred to the academic context, given that academic learning is so heavily 'book-driven' and entails learning what other people have codified rather than learning directly from one's own experience.

I therefore began to seek ways of incorporating teamwork into the curriculum at LSE. In 1999, following a chance encounter with a former colleague of mine, I was introduced to Ivan Kent, an experienced skills developer who had worked on the Enterprise in Higher Education programme and set up and run a Personal Development Programme (PDP) at another major London college. The PDP was a highly interactive, small-group-based skills development programme which provided training in teamwork, leadership, oral presentation, personal marketing and project management skills.

Ivan and I joined forces and got together with Dr Edgar Whitley of the Information Systems department at LSE, who regularly gave his MSc students a group project to undertake. The teamwork aspect of this was already strongly emphasized, and students were required to submit at the conclusion of the project an individual reflective report on their experience of teamwork. Ivan and I offered to contribute 'teamwork tutoring' modules to the course, designed to help students to work creatively and effectively as members of teams, and our offer was accepted. In exchange for our contribution, we were able to learn about the issues that arose in these teams and to try out and develop techniques to address these issues. We saw this as a process in which students were very much our collaborators rather than subjects. We have now been doing this for five years.

Since 2000 we have been able to work with other LSE departments too, notably Social Policy (Social Policy and Planning in Developing Countries) and the Interdisciplinary Institute of Management. And from 2000 to 2002 we were able to broaden our work into an action-research project on developing and marketing graduates' skills, supported by a grant from the DfEE/HEFCE Higher Education Innovations Fund.

I owe a particular debt of gratitude to all the students who have willingly welcomed myself and Ivan into their projects and lives, allowed us to witness them at work, and discussed problems and difficulties with us. My special thanks are due to Ivan Kent, my colleague and collaborator, to Graham Topping, and to Edgar Whitley, Sunil Kumar and Liz Barnett at LSE. I am also very grateful to Mike Rawlins, Peter Danby, Lis Dunne, Jane Measures, Liz Plumb, Serena Mackesy, Lesley Munro-Faure, Myszka Guzkowska, Anne-Marie Martin, Elaine Sinclair, Mike Tiley, Carol Baume and Rachel Segal, for stimulus, opportunities, encouragement and resources, in many forms.